It's Time *for* Joy!

Praise for *It's Time for Joy!*

"This wonderful book reveals the ***secret*** to creating a life of joy ***right now***! It inspires you to re-examine your values and will cause you to make decisions that will affect your future in a positive way. Become a source of lasting joy--rush out today and give copies to your family and friends."

Bob Proctor
Author, *The Secret* and *You Were Born Rich*

"Brian Biro not only knows what he's talking about, he's also an exquisite example of joy. This is indeed a joyful book, bursting with possibility and enthusiasm for a life of greater richness, meaning, and fulfillment. I loved reading it!"

John Robbins
Author, *Diet for a New America, May All Be Fed* and *Reclaiming Our Health*

"*It's Time for Joy* provides a simple yet compelling message of hope, love, and personal responsibility. Brian Biro's stories are powerful catalysts for reigniting one's passion for life."

John Gray
Author, *Men Are From Mars, Women Are From Venus*

"*It's Time for Joy* is full of 'chicken soup' for the human soul. In this wonderful book, Brian Biro has captured the essence of how to enjoy every precious moment of life."

Marci Shimoff
Author, *The Secret, Chicken Soup for the Woman's Soul,* and *Happy For No Reason*

"*It's Time for Joy* will lift your soul, ignite your spirit, and warm your heart. A great read!"

Ken Blanchard
Author, *The One-Minute Manager* and *Gung Ho!*

"Brian shares compelling stories and insights that have made him the most dynamic, inspiring, and loving seminar leader I have experienced. In *It's Time for Joy* he gives us ways that can enable us to 'enjoy every precious moment' also.

Marlene Hays
Publisher, *The Light Connection* Newspaper

"In these hectic days, we take time to feed our bodies and minds, but oftentimes neglect our souls. *It's Time for Joy* will replenish your soul, and you will discover the treasure we were all meant to enjoy—a life of happiness and purpose which is determined by choice, not chance."

John McCormack
Founder/CEO, Visible Changes, Author, *Self-Made in America*

"I enjoyed every precious moment reading *It's Time for Joy!* I found it to be a compelling guide that has awakened, inspired, and uplifted my heart like never before, making life more fulfilling. This wonderful book has allowed me to take these principles, share them with compassion, and inspire others to believe in themselves and to pursue their unlimited potential."

Paulette Kimura-Shimabukuro
Mother, Real Estate Entrepreneur, MLM champion

"My Joyful Spirit is ready to sing at the top of my lungs! This is a masterfully written how-to work of art. Now anyone can find their passion…Brian Biro has made it easy."

Karl Anthony
Singer, Songwriter

It's Time for Joy!

how to become
the happiest person you know

Brian D. Biro

New York

It's Time for Joy

How to Become the Happiest Person You Know

Second Edition

ISBN 978-1-60037-602-3

Library of Congress Control Number: 2009901767

MORGAN · JAMES
THE ENTREPRENEURIAL PUBLISHER

Morgan James Publishing, LLC
1225 Franklin Ave., STE 325
Garden City, NY 11530-1693
Toll Free 800-485-4943
www.MorganJamesPublishing.com

To the loving memory of my friend, Diana,
Who awakened me to a truth that has changed the direction, purpose, and meaning of my life:
The love we fail to share is the only pain we live with.

And to Carole, Kelsey, and Jenna, who fill my spirit with unbridled joy in every precious moment!

Contents

Introduction

Enjoy every precious moment!

These four words have become a basic creed for me, a reminder that this gift called life is truly an extraordinary honor and opportunity. Every letter I write and every voice-mail message I leave end with this simple statement. And nearly every day someone responds to these four words with sincere thanks because they awaken feelings of love, joy, and gratitude, shattering the numbness and "taking-for-granted" attitude that sometimes seep into our souls.

The decision to embrace every moment as a precious gift is ultimately a choice of love over fear. The impact of that choice can be so profound, so transformational, that it changes your perspective, your presence, and your peace of mind forever. You will see beauty, hope, and opportunity where you would have completely missed them before making this pivotal choice. You will find yourself connecting with people you might have avoided before, even the people you're pretty certain were put on the planet to "test" you. You will recognize that material possessions do not make the biggest difference; the spirit and heart you bring to each day ultimately determine the quality of your life and the lasting effect you have on others. This book will offer you new choices to enrich every moment—to build a truly joyful spirit.

Chapter 1
Diana's Dreams

When the phone rang that autumn morning, it startled me from my immersion in my world of kickboards, chlorine, workouts, and weight training. I had become so caught up in my role as head coach of one of the country's largest swimming teams that there was practically no room for anything else. I wondered who would be calling me at this time of the morning. Perhaps it was one of my assistant coaches seeking some advice or a parent with a question about our upcoming fund-raising project. I rarely heard from anyone outside my swimming circle. But when I picked up the phone, the voice on the line was warm yet unfamiliar.

"Is this Brian Biro?"

When I answered yes, she continued on purposefully. "I'm calling you this morning because an old friend of yours asked me to. Diana Smith wanted me to invite you to Mount St. Mary's on Saturday at three o'clock in the afternoon."

She paused for a moment as if to collect herself and then went on. "You see, Diana passed away last night."

The words cut into me like a knife. Hardly breathing as shock, disbelief, and pain converged to level my heart and soul, I fought to control my rising anguish as the voice continued gently. "She battled her cancer for many months before it finally took her. Diana wanted you to be with her children at her funeral. In her last days, she planned the entire service. Her wish was that it become a celebration of her life rather than a mourning of her death. I feel as though we've already met, because Diana told me so much about you. She said you had filled her with hope when she felt she was wasting her life. She wanted you to know how deeply your faith in her had affected her spirit. Will you come?"

With my mind racing and my stomach tied in knots, I managed to stammer in a near whisper, "Yes, I'll be there."

Weak, I thanked her and hung up the phone. I sat stunned, as if someone had knocked the wind out of me. How could this have happened? How could I have let seven years go by without speaking to Diana, without checking in on this extraordinary friend who had given so much to me? Why had she wanted me to be present at her funeral when I had been absent from her life for so long?

The days leading to the funeral were a blur of confusion and pain for me. I felt helpless and numb as I stumbled through my coaching routine. For the first time I could remember, I could barely focus on my swimmers.

I had met Diana when I was eighteen years old. In the summer before my sophomore year at Stanford, I'd worked as a swimming instructor in the San Fernando Valley. I still remember her gentle smile the first morning she brought her youngest son, David, to the pool for private swimming lessons with me. She was so proud of David and the progress he had made that summer advancing from fear to freestyle. He'd emerged more than water-safe; by the end of the summer he was a strong little swimmer.

The spring of my junior year, I made the decision to return to the San Fernando Valley for the summer to operate my own swim lesson business in backyard pools. I wrote to Diana and asked if she had an interest in David continuing his lessons. In less than a week, she sent me back a wonderful letter offering the use of her pool. Not only did she want me to continue with David, she was excited to have her two older children work with me to learn all of their competitive strokes, because they wanted to try out for the summer swim team. She didn't stop there. She had already lined up about eight private lessons with other families in her neighborhood and felt sure she could find more. Suddenly, thanks to Diana, my new business was off to a flying start!

My days that summer were packed with coaching in the early morning, followed by a full slate of lessons from nine to five-thirty, and, finally, three more hours of coaching. It was an intense schedule but incredibly fulfilling to watch the children grow so much in confidence and skill—not to mention the financial bonanza it produced for me. I needed every penny I could save for my Stanford tuition. In the midst of these fifteen-hour days, I really looked forward to my lessons at Diana's house. I loved working with her three children, fine-tuning their stroke techniques for the team. They were wonderful kids—bright, friendly, and eager to learn.

Every so often a cancellation would occur, leaving a twenty-minute opening in my schedule. In these brief interludes, Diana and I would talk about all kinds of subjects. She was truly interested in me and my education and took great delight as I described my friends and my life at Stanford. When she found out I was financing my own education through working and student loans, she stunned me by asking if she could send me some extra money to help with my school expenses. She was quite wealthy through family inheritance and told me she couldn't think of a better way to use some of her money. At first I told her I couldn't accept such a gift, but she was so reassuring and insistent that eventually I gave in. Over the next few years she sent me several thousand dollars I desperately needed. She was like my guardian angel. Gradually I began to know this remarkable woman, discovering that although she was perhaps the most giving person I had ever met, she was also one of the loneliest and least fulfilled. She had almost given up hope of ever doing so much she wanted to do in her life.

The sole sustaining joy in Diana's life was her children. She loved them completely. What's more, she truly admired them and reveled in their different personalities and ways of interacting with others. Erika, the oldest, was the intellectual. She was a grown-up at twelve—brilliant, logical, and so mature and serious Diana worried that Erika would miss the fun of learning to let go and play.

Craig, the middle child, was the lover. Gentle, empathetic, and deeply compassionate, he lived to make others happy. He was so like his mother that their expressions often looked like mirror-images of one another. Every day, Diana focused on ways to help Craig build faith and confidence in himself. She adored him and his giving spirit but was determined that he learn to receive, too, and to develop strength to balance his gentleness. She knew his happiness would ultimately depend upon his learning to love himself as well as others.

The youngest, David, was the character. With an imagination and impish wit that knew no bounds, he was creative and clever. Diana recognized immense talent in David but also saw a lack of discipline and determination to apply himself fully. She knew he hid behind his happy-go-lucky exterior. Her greatest wish for David was for him to know that, no matter the outcome of his efforts, the joy and fulfillment from giving one's best is one of life's greatest treasures.

The more we talked about the children, the more I began to see that Diana was in a very real sense raising them alone. Her relationship with her husband had gradually deteriorated into emptiness. He was an attorney who was rarely around. When he did come home, he'd settle into "a few tall ones" and television. He had little to do with the children or Diana. Having drifted apart long ago, they coexisted out of convenience.

One morning I arrived as usual at Diana's only to find that four of the children I taught were sick and had to cancel for the day. Since I had the rare gift of an hour and a half of free time, Diana invited me to join her for lunch out by the pool. As we sat down together, I began to ask about her for a change. We so often talked about the children and me; I was curious to learn more about this friend who had taken me under her gentle wings.

It was as if the gates had opened. Diana must have sensed that I was fully present with her and keenly interested in what she had to say, because she spilled her heart out to me. She knew her marriage was beyond repair; she had long since lost all feeling for her husband. She could no longer even be angry. All that remained was indifference. They lived completely separate, disconnected lives. She thought about leaving with the children but feared that it would hurt them. She knew Erika would be fine but worried that David was too young and Craig too sensitive to handle a broken home, so she stayed, devoting herself to her children and giving up all her other dreams.

And what dreams they were! She wanted to go back to school to earn her master's degree in psychology and perhaps a Ph.D. She loved to learn. She envisioned combining her passion for art and music with her study of behavioral psychology to help children with learning and emotional challenges.

As she spoke, I saw radiance in Diana I had never sensed before. She had always seemed so calm, but a tinge of sadness and resignation had always been present in her eyes. Now she bubbled with a passion for life that, for just a moment, rekindled hope within her.

I told her how amazing she was. "Why don't you go and live your dreams? You're an incredible mother and your children would love to see you find the same kind of happiness you want for them." I told her how much she deserved joy and that there was nothing she couldn't create in her life. I was twenty years old and filled with idealism and freedom. "The greatest gift you can ever give your children is to be an example of happiness."

A week or two later I returned to Stanford for my senior year. Diana continued to send me money with her wonderful letters. When she wrote, the same radiance I had seen that morning when she opened her life up to me jumped off the pages. I delighted in her letters.

That autumn was a time of real soul-searching for me. What was I going to do with my life? As much as I had enjoyed my education at Stanford, I realized that nothing brought me more joy than the coaching I did each summer. The inner satisfaction of helping children learn to truly believe in themselves was the greatest feeling I had ever experienced. Finally it became crystal clear to me that I would return to San Fernando Valley when I finished school to coach full time. I graduated a quarter early and made the move to my new adventure.

During my first week back, I went to visit Diana. When she met me at the door, her eyes welled up with tears. She hugged me tightly and I could feel her love. I had come to thank her for all she had given me, but her outpouring of emotion scared me. I didn't know how to handle being loved so intensely. I began to question whether she had given me so much because she wanted much more than my friendship in return. Suddenly I was terrified that she might have fallen in love with me.

And so I ran. As quickly as I could find an excuse to leave, I rushed out the door. When I reached my car, I looked back for just a moment at Diana still standing at the door. In my last glimpse of her, I saw enormous sadness. Somehow, she knew I was running away.

It took me years to see the truth—that her love was the most unconditional I had ever known. Her emotions that night had been pure gratitude and joy for her friend who had ignited fresh possibility that she could create her life rather than merely endure it. It was only my insecurity that had stirred my rising panic. I simply had not accepted myself enough to be so completely accepted by another.

These indelible memories swept through my soul as I drove to Mount St. Mary's seven years later on that Saturday afternoon. When I had run away from Diana, I'd kept right on running. I'd buried myself in my coaching, completely detaching myself from friends, family, and every part of myself except the role I played as coach. I'd seen Diana at the pool a few times but barely spoke to her, conveniently finding refuge in my rule about not conversing with anyone but the swimmers during practice. Never again did I stop by to visit and connect with my special friend. I thought about it many times, but always found myself "too busy" to take the time.

Now, I was on my way to her funeral.

As I walked into the chapel at Mount St. Mary's, I was met by three beautiful young adults—David, Craig, and Erika. They lit up when I arrived, running to me and throwing their arms around me. I hadn't seen them in many years, yet they made me feel like the most important person in the world. They escorted me to a seat in the very front of the chapel and then stunned me by sitting down beside me. We talked quietly as we waited for the service to begin and they told me what had happened to Diana.

She had died one of the happiest people on earth. All the dreams she had shared with me seven years before had come true—*she had made them come true.* She had taken a life of emptiness and resignation and transformed it into a masterpiece. After divorcing her husband, she and the kids had begun a new life together. She'd enrolled at UCLA and earned her Ph.D. in psychology. She'd had tremendous passion for her work with learning-impaired children and had rapidly become a rising star in her field.

As I listened to her children, I saw that Diana's vision and hopes for them had also become shining realities. Erika's brilliance and maturity were still immediately apparent, but she had become so *light!* Now a sophomore at Smith College, she had discovered how to let go and find joy even in the midst of difficult times. Craig's kindness and compassion were as unmistakable as ever, but I could sense an inner peace in him now. He was a young man who knew and liked who he was. And David, too, had found himself. He had become a fine student and athlete. He carried himself with strength and confidence. No longer the clown, he had become a person of substance and character. All three were intensely proud of their mother. She had always been their best friend, but as they had grown together, she had also become their hero.

When the cancer was discovered, all of them had been devastated and terrified, but Diana had remained positive and joyful to the last. She'd talked for hours with each of the children and told them these last years had been so rich and full that all she could feel was gratitude and joy. She'd let them know with every ounce of her enormous heart and spirit how deeply she loved and respected each of them. The experience of those years had helped Diana find a new spirituality and faith. She'd believed without question that she would always be with her children. Her body finally gave out, but her spirit lived on.

They had planned this day together. Each had chosen his or her part. During the service, Craig and David shared wonderful stories about Diana—how much fun they'd had together and how unconditionally she had trusted and believed in them—even when they'd stretched that faith to the limit. When they spoke, tears welled up, but they seemed much more tears of joy and triumph than tears of sadness and despair. Their mother had loved and been loved completely. There had been nothing more she'd wanted. She'd been truly happy.

At the end of the service, we were invited outside to a small courtyard in the center of Mount St. Mary's. It opened up to a brilliant blue sky that day. Each of us was handed a huge bouquet of brightly colored balloons as we stepped together into the courtyard.

Erika stood on a small bench and began to speak. "Mom wanted each of you to know how much you meant to her. She cherished your love and friendship. She envisioned you here today and wanted you to know that she is with us now. The balloons you hold represent the lightness, color, and energy you brought to her life. She asked that you remember the special moments you shared together as you look up at the balloons and then let them go. As they fly away, let go of any sadness or remorse and let all pain disappear just as the balloons fade from view. Know that when Diana left you, she was happier than she had ever been."

We watched together in silence as the balloons rose into that vivid blue sky, becoming tinier and tinier until all that was left was a memory. Yet we knew they were still out there floating on the wind. Finally Erika closed the ceremony when she said, "Now Mom wanted us to go inside together to eat pasta, listen to beautiful music, and drink champagne as we share in the celebration of her life."

That night I sat in the solitude of my apartment and began to write in my journal. As the thoughts swept from my mind and onto the pages, it was as if Diana was there with me, gently healing my tortured spirit. Slowly, I began to understand what she was trying to tell me by inviting me to be a part of this day. Seven years before I had run away from her, afraid she had fallen in love with me. Today, I had seen the truth—she loved *me*, my spirit, my hopefulness, and my belief in her possibilities. I had helped her choose to live rather than merely exist. She wanted me to know the impact that belief had created in her life and to feel her undying gratitude.

As I wrote that night, Diana reached into my soul and awakened my understanding that the ultimate choice we have been given is that between love and fear. I had helped her find the faith to choose love, and now she was helping me see that the lesson I had taught was the very one I most needed to learn. Only by choosing love can we discover abundance. Only by choosing love can we create joy. Only by choosing love can we *be loved*.

Diana's spirit fills every page of this book. Finding happiness is a matter of choice, not chance. As she chose love for herself, she became a shining example of energy and vitality for everyone she touched. She created a livelihood centered upon purpose and personal responsibility. Because of her new energy and purpose, every team of which she was a part, from her family to her clients to her professional colleagues, became enriched and more deeply connected. She threw open the window of opportunity—one we all have—to make her life a masterpiece and, as a result, made a magnificent difference for all of us lucky enough to have known her.

Diana made choices that transformed her vision and dreams into reality. Now it's time for you to embrace four simple choices to accelerate *your* life and create the joy you were meant to discover. Throughout this book, we will explore four areas of choice together that hold within them the opportunity for you to break free from the vice grip of doubt, lethargy, loneliness, and unfulfilled dreams. The actions you take from the ideas you'll develop as you move through these pages can save you from the intense, almost irremediable pain I carried with me for many years after losing Diana, because I did not understand the true preciousness of every moment. You will learn that there are only two true emotions—love and fear—and that a joyful spirit is the product of choosing love consistently with regard to your health and vitality, livelihood, relationships, and purpose. *Ultimately, the love we fail to share is the only pain we live with.* Within these simple yet enormously important areas of choice, you will discover the keys to pain-free living. Your reward will be a life of new happiness, and you will have the opportunity to become an example of energy, possibility, and hope.

Chapter 2
The Challenge of Change

Just as Diana discovered, igniting new joy requires *change*. It means you will embrace your birthright of personal leadership and make new decisions. Exercising fresh choices is not always easy. Decisions catapult us into the realm of the uncertain, as they move us from comfort zones into challenge zones. Yet only when you dive into these unknown waters can you make discoveries that elevate your spirit and expand your dimension as a human being.

It is particularly exhilarating right now to explore the challenge of change because we are in the midst of an extraordinary, accelerating time. Thanks to computer and telecommunications technologies, we have entered an information revolution. Humankind is expected to gather more than double the information in the next decade than we've accumulated in all recorded history! This explosion of new data reaches into our lives and affects us in myriad ways. In business we're seeing stunning changes because of these new technologies, from entire industries erupting and disappearing virtually overnight to an unprecedented migration to new forms of enterprise such as home-based businesses. Like the nineteenth-century settlers heading west in wagon trains, seeking fresh starts in a new land of freedom and opportunity, millions are setting out with determination and enthusiasm to take charge of their way of life. Our communication systems are at the forefront of these massive shifts in lifestyle and focus, with the Internet and World Wide Web suddenly supplying us with means to educate ourselves, shop, promote our products and services, network, and "visit" friends, family, and clients, all in the dimension of cyberspace. The barrage of accessible information has led us to eat differently, read differently, bank differently, exercise differently, and play differently than only a decade ago—and that's only a beginning. Soon we will see startling changes in many of the things we take for granted today, from travel to the way we access entertainment and professional services. Indeed, if there's one thing you can count on as we move deeper into this new millennium, it is *change*. Whether you fear it, seek to avoid it, or embrace it, change is coming—and coming fast.

So how do we deal with this escalating change and emerge with a joyful spirit? In the midst of this tumult, is it possible for us to develop genuine peace of mind? How can we create balance, confidence, and opportunity in the face of such turbulence? In his masterpiece, *Think and Grow Rich*, Napoleon Hill wrote, "With every adversity is planted the seed of an equivalent or greater benefit." There has never been a more ideal time to plant new seeds rich in hope, vitality, and contribution.

In this book you will learn about four such "super seeds"—key areas of choice filled with tremendous opportunities for every human being on this planet to discover greater happiness and fulfillment. These four key areas, or paradigms, give you a fresh context of where to direct and apply your initiative, vision, and passion. By setting your course to be a proactive champion—a master—in each of these four areas, you will discover countless benefits that can bring you success and inner satisfaction physically, emotionally, mentally, spiritually, and even financially.

Understanding Paradigms

What's your vision of our world as we move further into this new millennium? What significant changes are coming, and how can you prepare for them to positively affect you and those you love? These are tremendously "enabling" questions; as opposed to the often "disabling" questions we ask ourselves and others.

- **Disabling questions** direct our focus to that which we do not want—to what is wrong with ourselves and the world. They often begin with negative presuppositions such as, *Why don't you ever . . .?* or *Why are you so . . .?*
- **Enabling questions,** on the other hand, spur us to focus clearly and specifically on what we *do* want—leading to answers filled with possibility and opportunity.

The choices we make in each of the four crucial areas, which I've called "super seeds" and "paradigms," will assist us in creating new, empowering paradigms for ourselves filled with expanded possibilities for happiness and fulfillment. **You will discover greater success, fun, connection, and purpose than you've ever dreamed of as you take charge of your life in each of the key areas of *energy, livelihood,* the *relay paradigm,* and the *window of opportunity.*** But, before we explore them, let's have some fun getting really clear about what a paradigm actually is.

A paradigm, very simply, is your model of the world: how you look at things. The easiest way to understand it is to consider what happens when major changes occur, causing what's been called a *paradigm shift.*

I experienced a striking paradigm shift several years ago when I visited a spot where my family had vacationed when I was a little boy. I hadn't been back to Echo Lake since I was seven years old, yet my memories of our vacations at the beautiful, crystalline, blue oasis above the Tahoe Basin were incredibly vivid. In my childhood, the walk from the parking lot at the east end of the lake to our little cabin had felt like a marathon hike to my seven-year-old legs. Our cabin had seemed a grand and expansive mountain mansion. When I returned after a thirty-year hiatus, I thought, *Whoa, is this the same place?* The "marathon hike" covered no more than half a mile. The "mansion" was a tiny cabin with perhaps twelve hundred square feet. Everything I recalled as being so gigantic had magically shrunk. My vision of the world had changed radically—I had experienced a paradigm shift.

Another huge paradigm shift occurs for many of us when we become parents. Suddenly, our decisions and actions are affected because of this new frame of reference. We laugh about things, worry about things, and become alert to things we never even noticed before. When we adopt this parental paradigm, we awaken to the fact that we are truly examples to our children. The way we respond to problems and adversity, the tenderness and care we demonstrate to our children and one another, even our daily habits and how we use our time, all send powerful messages that become imprinted in our youngsters' minds.

What Causes Paradigm Shifts?

Sometimes paradigms undergo massive shifts because of dynamic changes in technology. Think of the impact of television, for example, on our collective perspective. Television has changed the lives of millions of people, from children to great-grandparents. When we recognize that the average child in the United States watches about forty-two hours of television per week, and the average father spends less than eight minutes per day in real interaction with his children, we begin to see the dramatic impact of this paradigm shift. Not only has the *content* of television programming affected our perceptions of ourselves and society, the *process of watching television* has moved us away from a more active, connective, and participative lifestyle.

Here's another striking example of a technology-driven paradigm shift. It's stunning to realize that before 1980 there were no personal computers. This technology has enabled us to organize, store, and utilize information previously far too cumbersome and time consuming to consider trying to manage. From accounting and budgeting systems, to the Internet, to database and spreadsheet programs, and multi-media applications, PCs have created a whole new set of possibilities and challenges in our lives. And, with the extraordinary advances in speed, storage, and ease of use, personal computing is in the midst of its own ongoing revolution.

Other sparks that can ignite paradigm shifts are new choices we make or experiences that affect us so deeply that we no longer view the world as we did before. For example, if we decide to stop working for someone else and start our own business, we experience a startling change in our paradigms. The same thing can happen for people who have overcome near-fatal illnesses or injuries. They see life differently, with new awareness that every moment is precious.

Major-impact events in our lives can dramatically affect how we view ourselves and our world. For example, **have you ever had somebody tell you something, do something for you, or treat you in such a way that it absolutely changed the way you felt about yourself, completely altering your overall confidence and perspective?**

My high school counselor, Mr. Anderson, once said to me, "You know, Brian, a student like you comes along only every ten or fifteen years." Now, when he said it, he could have meant it either positively *or* negatively! But I received it as a statement of heartfelt belief in my capabilities. As a result, from that point forward I looked at myself differently. He helped me discover a fresh new world of possibility for myself.

New thoughts and experiences I encountered when I wrote my first book, *Beyond Success*, caused me to change some of my paradigms. Up until that time, my work patterns had been based on speed. I did everything quickly. During the process of writing *Beyond Success*, however, I found I needed to develop far more patience than I had ever required of myself. There were days when I would sit for hours without typing a single word into my computer. At first, this was exasperating and discouraging. But after a few weeks of determined effort, I made an exciting new discovery: I could look at those days with great enthusiasm because I knew I was "percolating." Though momentarily stuck, I began to develop great confidence that the next day or even the next hour it would all come together. I gradually transformed what had been a paradigm of confusion and frustration into one of confidence and faith.

The Essence of a Paradigm

Now that we've examined some examples of shifting paradigms, how do we change ours to move beyond limits and open up new ways of finding greater happiness, confidence, and peace of mind? We create new perspectives by making fresh choices. And it's important to know that *now* is the time to make choices that serve you and accelerate your progress toward a truly joyful spirit. What follows is a classic story that serves as a wonderful metaphor for the value of identifying positive paradigms.

Once there was a group of nomads who wandered through the desert for many years in search of insight from a celestial source to guide them to the Promised Land. One evening as they set camp, they found themselves surrounded by a breathtaking white light. They stood spellbound and silent, wondering what would happen next. Then a great celestial voice spoke to them.

The voice said, "Go out around you and gather all the pebbles you can from the ground. Put them in your saddlebags. Then travel to your next camp. And tomorrow when you set camp, you will be both glad and sad."

With that, the great celestial voice spoke no more, and the light disappeared.

At first the nomads stood in stunned and silent contemplation. But after a few moments they became a little irritated as they talked to one another. After all, they had been wandering for years in search of this great message, and all they were told to do was pick up a bunch of rocks! It was ridiculous and demeaning, they thought, and they weren't going to do it. But then they remembered how strong the voice had been, and they thought, *Well, maybe we'd better just cover our bases.* So, just to be safe each of them gathered two or three pebbles. They stuffed the pebbles into their saddlebags and forgot about them until setting camp the next night. Then the nomads remembered what the voice said and reached into their saddlebags. As they pulled out the pebbles their eyes nearly popped out of their heads. What had previously been worthless little rocks had been magically transformed into magnificent diamonds!

At first the nomads were incredibly glad. They exclaimed, "We're rich! We're rich!" But then they were incredibly sad because they realized they had missed the opportunity to fill their saddlebags with thousands of these magic pebbles.

The empowering paradigms you will develop by making new choices in the four key areas at the heart of a joyful spirit are just like those magic pebbles, so fill your saddlebags! Each offers opportunities for you to get more happiness out of life and to give more to everyone you touch.

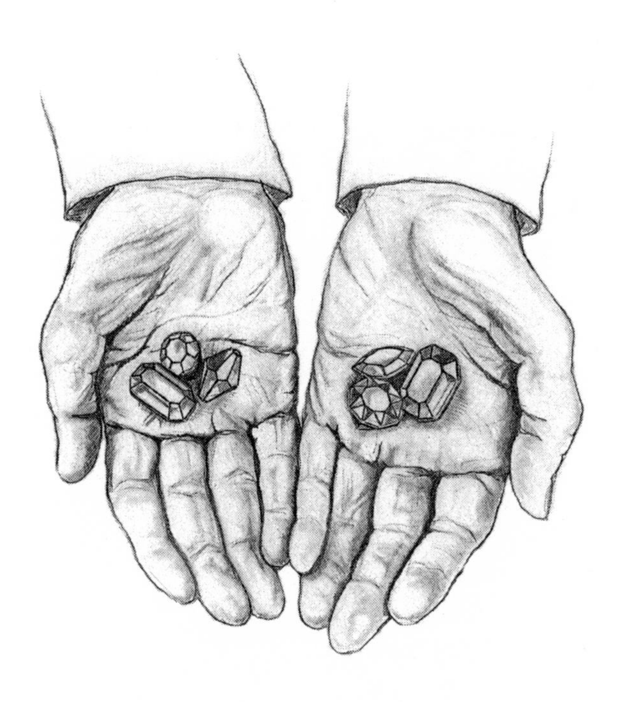

Chapter 3
Elevate Your Energy With Greater Health

In *Beyond Success* I revealed the underlying key to living your life "on purpose," to keeping yourself on track with your true intent. That key is *energy*. Increasing your understanding of energy is a magic pebble with the capacity to invigorate every moment of your life.

Right now we are faced with an *internal* energy crisis of huge proportion. Most of us think of our own physical energy the same way we think about the weather. We think, *Boy, I sure hope it's a sunny day for the family picnic this weekend. I hope I'm up for that meeting today.* We've fallen into the trap of thinking our energy level is something outside our control. But we can cultivate and build our energy by choice and not by chance.

Think of the people you most admire, people who seem to bring light to everyone they meet. They may not be flashy or flamboyant. They may be young or old, famous or unknown, wealthy or poor, outgoing or quiet. Whatever their race, creed, profession, or gender, there is one foundational element the people we most admire have in common. They are alight with "E-power"—glowing from the inside with enthusiasm, eagerness, and unstoppable energy—and you can be, too!

Just for fun, try this exercise right now. Wherever you are, sit up really tall. Straighten your backbone. Put a big toothy grin on your face for a second, and open your eyes a little wider. Now, fill yourself up with a rich, deep breath. Did you feel a rush of energy surging inside you? Emotion is created by motion, and you've just felt the truth of that adage. Suddenly, just by sitting up, changing your facial expression, and taking a rich, energizing breath, billions of cells in your body received new messages filled with vibrancy, creating the instantaneous result of heightened vitality and alertness. If we can transform our energy level so quickly simply by deciding to use our bodies differently, **imagine what we can do if we *consistently* make better choices about our health, our nutrition, and our physical vitality.**

When you consider that our bodies are made of remarkable building blocks called cells, which regenerate continuously (from three months for red blood cells to five days for muscle cells), you'll discover a whole new level of hope for building greater health and energy. That's why expanding your energy paradigm is so important! After all, you'll be practically a brand-new "you" eighteen months from now, with a body made of newborn cells. So the choices you make right now about nutrition and lifestyle are truly magic pebbles. Are you going to weigh yourself down with worthless rocks or energize yourself with magical diamonds that can transform your level of vitality?

Draw on the Best of Both Medical Science and Your Own Natural Healing Ability

A powerful way to generate consistently improved energy is to draw the absolute best from two different paradigms of health—the classical medical model, founded on western science, and the increasingly popular natural healing model, founded on ancient eastern teachings. Each model has value and offers distinct benefits, and you can exercise your choice to derive the best from both. Let's explore how doing so can protect you and help you achieve vibrant energy and health.

First, though, we need to take a look at who is ultimately in charge. In *Beyond Success*, I introduced a fun and extremely important concept I learned from a personal development teacher, Lou Tice. The principle was about "who-saids of the greatest magnitude." Remember the children's classic, *The Wizard of Oz*? It's really a great story about a who-said of the greatest magnitude.

In *The Wizard of Oz*, Dorothy had been blown over the rainbow and wanted to get back home to Kansas. She ended up in a magical land filled with Munchkins, an Emerald City, and all kinds of wild things. When she met the Munchkins and Glinda, the Good Witch of the North, they told her she needed to go see the Wizard of Oz. He was a who-said of the greatest magnitude, so off she went in search of the wizard.

Along the way to Oz, as she traveled down the yellow brick road, Dorothy encountered a scarecrow that didn't have a brain. She encountered a tin woodsman who didn't have a heart, and she encountered a lion who was just a big coward—he didn't have any courage. She recruited them as her teammates, and along with her little dog, Toto, they journeyed together to the Emerald City in the kingdom of Oz.

After a series of adventures, they finally came face to face with the wizard. It was then that the wizard really became a who-said of the greatest magnitude.

With great pomp and ceremony to demonstrate his unquestioned authority, he said to the scarecrow, "Here, scarecrow, by the power vested in me as a great and powerful wizard I give you this diploma! Now you're smart. Go act like it." And the scarecrow did.

Then the wizard said to the tin woodsman, "You had no heart before, but by the power vested in me as a great and powerful wizard, I give you this clock that ticks. We'll have it installed inside your tin casing and you'll have a heart! Go out and feel love and emotion." And the tin woodsman did.

Then the wizard stood before the cowardly lion and said, "By the power vested in me as a great and powerful wizard, and because of the tremendous bravery you exhibited in helping Dorothy bring back the broomstick from the Wicked Witch of the West, I hereby give you this medal of courage. You are now brave. Go act like it." Instantly the lion was no longer cowardly but was transformed into the king of the forest.

At the end of the story, we learn that the wizard has no real magical powers at all, yet the scarecrow becomes smart, the tin woodsman becomes loving, and the lion becomes courageous. **Such is the transformative power of a who-said of the greatest magnitude.** A who-said is someone we respect so highly, in whom we place such faith, that what they say, we do. And eventually, what they say we are, we become.

In our culture we have several who-saids. For example, many people go to see a who-said called a priest, minister, pastor, or a rabbi. Before that day, they lived like single people, acting quite single. Then all at once, the who-said says (usually with great ceremony), "By the power vested in me, I now pronounce you married. Go and act married." And they do. The who-said says it just once and it happens. That's the power we give to very strong who-saids.

One of today's most powerful who-saids is a physician. In many cases, that can be beneficial. Most doctors are deeply caring, highly intelligent, and wise human beings. In the medical model, your doctor is the ultimate and final who-said about your health. But stop and think for a second.

If you want to achieve constantly better health and vitality, another who-said must step up to the plate. That who-said of the greatest magnitude is *you*! For no matter how knowledgeable and educated a physician may be, you are the only one who knows exactly how you feel inside. That's why your choices count. So how do you best exercise those choices to become your own wellness coach—supported by, but not dependent upon, the professional health practitioners you choose to consult? You can begin by looking at the foundational premises and commonsense applications of both the medical model and the natural healing model. Then you can make educated choices that will skyrocket your level of consistent energy.

The Real Difference Between the Established Medical Model and the Natural Healing Model

The medical model is designed to treat symptoms. Fundamentally, our Western medical system shifts into gear only *after* you're already sick or injured. That's why, when it comes to crises such as broken bones, a collapsed lung, or clogged and constricted arteries, the medical model shines. But it's really startling to realize that nearly two-thirds of the total dollars expended in the United States on health care are spent during a patient's last six weeks of life. I don't know about you, but for me, that's way too late! That's why the natural healing model makes such great sense in balance with the medical model. Natural healing is all about *prevention*: It's designed to work on underlying causes. While the medical model is basically reactive and responsive (except for physical examinations, which are wonderful additions to the western system), the natural healing model is dynamically proactive.

Here's how the two paradigms relate. In the medical model, the basic tools for treating symptoms are synthetic drugs. Sometimes these drugs create side effects which require you to take other drugs to treat them. Then you might need to take a few more drugs to treat the side effects of the drugs for the side effects. Pretty soon you can fill up several medicine cabinets. Conversely, **the natural healing model is based on a simple belief in the ability of our bodies to heal themselves when we give them the raw materials they need.** That's why the natural healing model focuses on nutrition rather than drugs. Its proponents believe in giving the body great nutrition, such as raw organic foods and essential minerals as primary sources of abundant energy, exercise, a super attitude, and plenty of rest so that it will naturally work toward great natural health and balance. This principle is called *homeostasis*.

John Robbins, author of *Diet for a New America, May All Be Fed,* and *Reclaiming Our Health,* has said that no matter how hard we try, we simply can't duplicate the wisdom of nature in a test tube or laboratory. That makes great sense and has fueled my determination to search out the best possible sources of quality nutrition. It also explains why a rapidly increasing number of people are carefully reading labels and seeking to bring more wild and organic foods into their diets. They want to make sure that foods free of pesticides, artificial preservatives, and synthetic chemicals make up a larger portion of their diets.

In the last fifty years, we've seen a devastating increase in the incidence of degenerative diseases—ailments such as heart disease, cancer, and arthritis. These aren't contagious diseases; you develop them over time through choices you make about diet, exercise, and attitude that don't serve your body's vital systems.

The Three Fundamentals of Natural Healing

Finding and using the very best sources of super-nutrition—sources rich in trace minerals that are no longer prevalent in our depleted soils; sources alive with natural and easily assimilated vitamins and enzymes, amino acids, and beta-carotene; sources that provide the wonderful blood-purifying benefits of chlorophyll—enable the body to perform three fundamental, ongoing actions we need for dynamic energy.

- **The first of these functions is *cleansing*.** We must constantly cleanse the system of wastes and toxins such as polluted air and water, empty foods, pesticides, chemical additives, preservatives, and the physical by-products of stress, pressure, and tension. With healthy cleansing occurring continuously, we next need to consume foods that truly nourish us.
- ***Nourishment* is the second of the natural healing functions**, and it allows the third key action to take place, which is *vibrant generation of healthy new cells.* That's what the natural healing model is all about: cleansing, nourishment, and generation.

The Transformational Power of Heightened Energy

When you apply this understanding of the Western medical model and the natural healing model by deciding to accept the different gifts each has to offer, the results can be truly transformational. Our family has a very special friend, Jamie, who has always been an energetic, vivacious person. Her upbeat and outgoing personality makes her a joy to be around. She teaches fourth grade, where a high level of energy is mandatory for survival! Jamie has a wonderful family with two young sons and a husband who, along with being a terrific human being, is an exceptionally active outdoorsman. Jamie loves to ski, run, and exercise. She and her family spend much of their time enjoying the wonders of nature and a vibrant life.

A few years ago, however, that lifestyle came to a screeching halt as Jamie developed nearly debilitating arthritis. On most days she was in such agony in her joints, ankles, and feet that it took every ounce of her energy just to get out of her chair. She could no longer exercise and, worse, her attitude began to gradually sink as if in quicksand.

Teaching became a daily struggle because she was in so much pain. She felt trapped in an irreversible downward spiral, doubting if she would ever have any kind of quality of life again. Knowing she could no longer participate hurt deeply as she watched her husband and sons play together outside, running, laughing, and having fun.

Jamie refused to give up, though, and began to look for new answers. She sought to balance the gifts from both the medical and natural healing models. She decided to change her diet, replacing nutrient-deficient foods with new choices to improve her level of overall nutrition. And she really worked on her attitude. She teamed with her physician to wean herself from drug therapy and medication. As she improved, she utilized the advanced technological testing procedures provided by western science to measure her progress. The results were amazing. By meshing the best from both models, Jamie improved dramatically. Today she's back to being Jamie. She can run. She can ski again. She recently returned from two weeks in the Caribbean, where she snorkeled, laughed, and played on the beach with her family. Teaching is once again a passion rather than a punishment. Most of all, she has rediscovered the joy, connection, and purpose she feared were lost forever.

This kind of transformation is possible when you seize the opportunity inherent in this first pivotal area in which to build a joyful spirit. To help you get started toward consistently greater vitality, here is a valuable exercise designed to elevate your level of energy on a daily basis.

The "E-meter"

Begin this simple yet extremely powerful exercise by measuring your energy level on your own ten-point "E-meter" (energy scale), with one being completely exhausted, and ten being as energized and vibrant as you feel when you're doing something you absolutely love. Take a personal E-meter reading three times a day for one week and mark it on the energy chart. Take the first reading in the morning, the second around midday, and the third in the evening. Jot down any observations or thoughts about the factors you notice affecting your energy.

After a week, look at your E-meter chart to receive the answer to a question absolutely pivotal to the quality of your life: *At what energy level are you living?* You'll see graphically whether your energy level is fairly consistent or if you have widely disparate peaks and valleys.

Check Your E-Meter 3 Times Daily!

Give yourself an honest rating of your "E"nergy level:

1 = *"I can't get off the couch."*

5 = *"I can move, but my energy's kinda low."*

10 = *"I'm so pumped, I could jump-start your car!"*

This Week	Morning Reading	Midday Reading	Evening Reading
Day 1	______	______	______
Day 2	______	______	______
Day 3	______	______	______
Day 4	______	______	______
Day 5	______	______	______
Day 6	______	______	______
Day 7	______	______	______

Next Month	Morning Reading	Midday Reading	Evening Reading
Day 1	______	______	______
Day 2	______	______	______
Day 3	______	______	______
Day 4	______	______	______
Day 5	______	______	______
Day 6	______	______	______
Day 7	______	______	______

Recently a lovely young woman attended one of my seminars for the second time. During one session we played three energy games designed to help participants recognize the remarkable degree of choice they have in cultivating greater energy. I ended the session by asking participants to estimate the levels at which they were living their lives on their personal E-meters, and who ultimately determined their energy levels. The question ignited a sudden "aha" in this young woman, and she couldn't wait to tell me about her insight.

She began by explaining what she had learned from the first seminar. She said, "Three years ago when I attended your seminar, the greatest gift I received was new clarity about what I really wanted in my life. For the first time I knew my highest priority. Over the two-and-a-half days, I became focused and deeply inspired by a vision of building a family. At the time, I was single, not involved in any meaningful relationship, and unaware of how much I longed for the love and connection of family. It's so exciting to come back to your seminar now, because six months ago today, my husband and I welcomed a miracle into our lives—our baby daughter!"

Then she went on to explain what she had just discovered about her E-meter. "It was so much fun to play the energy games, but when you asked where we're living on our ten-point E-meters, I suddenly realized something really important. You see, at work, I'm 'on,' flying around the office at level eight or nine consistently. But then I go home—to my dream—and I drop to about level three. Now I know that I have a choice. I like my energy and focus at work, and now I'm determined to build my energy at home for my husband and daughter. I'm so excited—I can hardly wait to see them tonight!"

Imagine what would happen to the quality of your life if you simply elevated your consistent E-meter reading by one full point. When you're filled with energy you're more flexible, alert, and enthusiastic. You're able to deal with change more easily and positively, and your impact on others is immediately heightened. Once you've measured yourself for a full week on your E-meter, you'll be able to set some empowering goals for changes and improvements. The next step is to conscientiously apply three fundamental keys to building greater energy over the next thirty days and then take another reading on your E-meter. Through your focus and action, you will be rewarded with new vitality—the springboard to a richer quality of life!

The Three Keys to Building Greater Energy

Think of how tremendous you would feel springing to life each morning with all the energy you need to handle whatever challenges come your way. Now that you've established your new personal E-meter goals, this kind of vibrancy is possible for you when you take action in each of the three keys to greater energy—*diet*, *movement*, and *a compelling why.* Decide which areas offer you the greatest opportunity for improvement and set yourself on a new course for the next thirty days by designing a personal vitality game plan.

Key #1: Diet

The first key to building greater vitality is adopting a diet that supports you in feeling light and energized at a cellular level. You've seen from our examination of the natural healing model that your diet must provide the essential raw material to sustain energy over the long haul. By consciously eating a variety of wholesome, nutrient-rich foods, you allow your body to find the natural balance and harmony that was intended for it. If you've been run-down, eating a poor diet of fatty and highly processed foods, or feeling stressed and fatigued, your body is already screaming out for cleansing and nourishment. Adopting a diet rich in fresh vegetables, fruits, whole grains, and legumes (especially homegrown or organically farmed); drinking plenty of fresh juices and pure water, and supplementing your diet with super foods loaded with natural trace minerals, amino acids, and chlorophyll are your best offense against disease and your greatest support for a strong and healthy immune system. A diet rich in these nutritious foods also assists efficient cleansing. Thus, your first step in designing your vitality game plan is to examine and improve your diet. Even small changes can create dynamic results.

Next, take a look at the *quantity* of food you are eating. Often, simply reducing your portions at each meal by ten or twenty percent can make a remarkable difference in your energy level. Most Americans are overfed but undernourished. Making the simple decision to chew your food five more times with each bite is another powerful way to improve health. This habit of chewing your food more will markedly increase the enzymatic activity that enhances your digestion. The result is a feeling of lightness and energy.

Key #2: Movement

The second key to cultivating greater energy is *movement*. It has been said that people don't really grow old—they just stop moving. Think of the times in your life when you were actively engaged in some form of regular exercise and physical movement. Was your experience of life richer and more satisfying? Did you feel more alert mentally? When challenges arose were you more flexible and at peace emotionally?

Think back to our little experiment when I asked you to sit up straighter, take a rich, full breath, and put a huge grin on your face. The surge of energy you felt occurred because you changed your physiognomy, which instantly altered your biochemistry. Suddenly billions of cells were flooded with new information and fresh stimulation. This is why movement is the single fastest way to change your emotions and help you get back on track with energy and purpose. All of us have had days when we felt so exhausted we didn't think we could move off the sofa. Completely drained, we couldn't even muster the energy to make it from the couch to the bedroom. But have you ever been in that kind of near-comatose state when something suddenly startled you? Perhaps your child cried out or there was an unexpected knock at the door.

Boom! Your E-meter flew off the chart and you sprang into action with a level of energy you thought impossible only moments before.

Movement and exercise also stimulate your creativity, recharging you when you feel stifled or blocked. As an example, for decades I have been a dedicated runner. Each time I go for a run I feel my spirit soar. I relax into a state where I let go of trying to force answers and instead allow a quiet, natural integration to take place. Ideas and concerns that have been swirling about helter-skelter within me seem to settle into a workable order. Inevitably when I return, I am rejuvenated and inspired. If I've been stuck on a problem, suddenly I am back in motion, seeing new possibilities and feeling new hope.

So look for ways to get up and moving. Turn off the television set. Step away from that computer. Walk or bike rather than driving the car for errands around your neighborhood. One of the very best ways to ignite greater movement in your life is to establish a regular exercise routine. By increasing your daily movement, you'll enhance your feelings of balance, clarity, and vibrancy.

How can you create an exercise plan that really works for you? Many people have great intentions of exercising regularly only to see their plans fade away because of too many obligations and too little time. But the rewards from regular exercise are enormous, beginning with increased physical energy, stamina, and flexibility, to greater ease in handling adversity, and increased peace of mind and inner satisfaction. Here are three simple principles to help you establish a program that keeps you on track and activated.

- **First, decide whether you prefer exercising alone or with others.** For many, the key to regular exercise is the social outlet provided by a YMCA, health or racquet club, a masters' swimming program, martial arts courses, aerobic classes, or simply running or lifting weights with a buddy. The fun and interaction of joining with others creates the ongoing inspiration to stick with an exercise plan until it becomes habitual. I know many people with graveyards of exercise equipment in their garages or basements who would be happily involved in regular fitness activity if they simply recognized that working out with others was a pivotal motivation for them.

- **Second, use the *principle of progression.*** For exercise and movement to become a basic part of everyday life, it must become habitual. Generally it takes thirty days of conscious, consistent action to build a new habit. If over the course of those thirty days you see genuine progress being made physically, emotionally, and mentally from your chosen exercise program, you will have a far greater likelihood of sticking with it. You'll establish the habit of that exercise program as a vital part of your day. For example, when I first began running, I was in poor physical shape. I ran a total of four minutes the first time out and thought I was going to keel over, but each day following that initial "marathon," I used the principle of progression to heighten my inspiration. My plan was very simple. I ran one more minute on the front half of my route for that day, which meant I ran two full minutes more by the time I returned home. I progressed to six minutes on my second day, eight on the third, ten on the fourth, and so on. Within two weeks, I was running over half an hour without stopping. My weight began to drop and my energy and spirit rose. By the end of my first thirty days, I had built up to over an hour of continuous running, and I was hooked!
- **Third, choose an exercise time that works for you.** Some people thrive on an early-morning exercise program. It revs their engine for the day and sets them off feeling alert and on track. For others, setting aside time during the lunch hour is optimal. Those who prefer this noon routine feel

reenergized for the afternoon and evening. The exercise breaks their day in half, giving them an opportunity to let go, integrate the events of the morning, and allow a plan for the afternoon to gently come into focus. Evening is the perfect workout time for those who use their exercise programs to decompress and release the tensions of their day. After a day of meetings, sitting in an office, talking on the phone or staring at a computer screen, the opportunity to move and exercise is wonderfully rejuvenating. Choose the pattern that feels natural, motivating, and satisfying for you. If it feels like you have to force yourself, try a different time until you find what works best for you.

Chapter 4
The Ultimate Key to Ongoing Energy—Your Compelling Why

The third and most important key to activating your energy is defining and developing a truly *compelling why*—a deeply inspiring purpose for the choices you make about how to live your life. Diana's expanded purpose transformed her life from fear to freedom, from failure to faith, and the same will manifest for you when you zero in on your compelling why. In his book *The On-Purpose Person*, Kevin W. McCarthy begins his final chapter with a wonderful quote from Norman Vincent Peale that captures the heart of living with a compelling why. "Every person is born for a purpose. Everyone has a God-given potential, in essence, built into them. And if we are to live life to its fullest, we must realize that potential."

One Thanksgiving, my dear friend, John Navazio, shared a story with me that vividly portrayed the transformational power of a compelling why to ignite energy and to keep the fire of purpose burning over the long term. John's father abandoned his family before John was born, so he was raised by his mother and grandmother. When he was two years old, his grandmother took on the responsibility of caring for Johnny while his mother went to work full time to make ends meet.

She was with him when he woke up each morning and, many nights, stayed with him until he was asleep because John's mother worked late. At seventy years of age, it was as if she had become a mother all over again.

Granny was John's primary parent throughout his childhood. In his last year of high school, they sat down together one evening and talked about their years together. She told John that when he was almost two, she had become extremely ill and fallen into a coma, teetering between life and death for several days. She'd found out later that her doctors had strongly doubted she would pull through. But from deep in the darkness, a dream and a vision had brought her back—her purpose unfulfilled. In her dream she had seen Johnny crying, alone in a dark corner. Then a brilliant white light had shone on him and a voice had told her, "Johnny needs you. You can't go." The next thing she remembered was the doctor smiling at her as he checked her pulse and breathing.

The memory of the dream was so vivid, it never left her. The dream had given her a compelling why, an energizing purpose to rise each morning and make the most of each day. Those years of caring for her grandson had been as meaningful and rewarding as any she had experienced in a rich and full life. As she told John about this, she was eighty-six years old, still sharp, alert, and vibrant. Tears welled up in her eyes when she revealed, "It was you and your mother who gave me a reason to go on. I thought I was all used up, that I had finished what I had been put here for. But you both needed me and I couldn't go. That purpose gave me life."

Your personal compelling why is the most pivotal of the three keys to building extraordinary energy. Without it, you will likely fall into the black hole of procrastination and indecision. Gradually you may feel your sense of self-worth shrivel as you become resigned to merely existing rather than truly living. With a compelling why, you will overcome seemingly insurmountable obstacles with energy you never knew you possessed. You will have taken a quantum leap toward becoming a master of the Energy Paradigm.

Identifying Your Compelling Why

To begin the process of developing a clear, compelling why in your life, you must look at your core beliefs, values, and emotions. Here is a simple and powerful three-step exercise to first identify and then ignite and reinforce your compelling why on a daily basis. The relatively small amount of time invested in participating fully in this process will open fresh opportunities for you to discover greater abundance, joy, and purpose than you've ever known.

Step 1: Discovering Your Greatest Passion

Begin by writing down your answers to the following questions. If you prefer, you can have a close friend or family member interview you, using the questions, and tape record the answers so you can transcribe them later. Choose whichever method appeals to you most. Remember, the answers you're looking for must come from deep in your heart and spirit. Find a quiet and peaceful place to complete this exercise, free of distractions.

Before you start, take five deep, full breaths, and be sure to exhale completely; allow your body to thoroughly relax. When you're ready, let yourself become fully associated to the questions. Put yourself into the times and places that come up for you as if you were actually there now. This is the key to moving beyond your superficial answers into your deeper thoughts, exposing what you truly believe.

Questions to Uncover Your Compelling Whys

1. When in your life have you felt nearly unstoppable, filled with energy, focus, and zest? What specifically were you doing?
2. What specifically has almost irresistible interest for you? About what subject do you want to read, learn, and devour every piece of available information?
3. What fills you up with feelings of joy and inner satisfaction?
4. If you knew you had only one year left to live, what would be most important for you to accomplish?
5. Who means the most to you? How do you feel about these people? What do they inspire in you?
6. What would you do with full-out energy if you knew you couldn't fail?

7. What is the greatest team you've ever been a part of?
8. What made it such a great team?
9. How did you feel to be a part of that team?
10. What was your special contribution to that team?
11. What is the greatest gift you will ever give? Who is the gift for and what will it mean?

Your answers to these questions enable you to identify the people, events, areas of interest, and emotions that fill you with the greatest passion. By answering the questions, you step away from habitual patterns, escaping the taking-for-granted attitude, to develop new clarity about your priorities. These answers will serve another important purpose in Step 2, where you will use them as raw material to create powerful statements called *abundance affirmations.*

Step 2: Creating Abundance Affirmations

By immersing yourself fully in the process of answering the compelling why questions, you've created an exciting next step: the opportunity to transform the key realizations you've discovered into *abundance affirmations.* These are empowering statements of absolute intention, faith, and unconditional love. All great thinkers I have ever known or studied understood and used the power of affirmation to move in the direction of their vision. Affirmations may take many forms, from prayers to mission statements to personal oaths or creeds. All affirmations share a common goal—to direct focus toward that which you truly want rather than that which you don't want. That simple shift in the direction of your focus can become one of the most life-changing decisions you will ever make.

The special affirmations you will create using the insights gained from the questions below will be written in a form that adds extraordinary energy to each statement. I call them abundance affirmations because they help you shift away from feelings of scarcity and doubt to an abundance mentality filled with possibility and faith. I have been electrified by the results of writing and then visualizing these abundance affirmations in my own life.

The process of writing abundance affirmations is simple yet taps into divine energy because it uses your ability to focus on three of life's greatest gifts—free choice (intention), possibility (openness to receiving), and understanding (an inner knowledge that the possibilities you choose for yourself are real and achievable). As you write and then visualize your abundance affirmations, you will feel a connection to unconditional divine love. This connection helps you accelerate the transformation of your abundance affirmations from vision to reality.

Here are basic guidelines for writing abundance affirmations.

1. **Begin by looking closely at your answers** to the compelling-why questions. Write down the keywords you use to describe the emotions, actions, primary areas of interest, contributions you wish to make to others, achievements, and relationships that are most important to you. These will become apparent as you read through your compelling-why answers. Use these keywords as you write your abundance affirmations.

> Example: Here is my keyword list from the answers to the compelling-why questions: *acceleration, love, insight, empowerment, ultimate family-building guide, purpose, beautiful home and retreat center, financial abundance, grow, learn, open, quiet, beauty, fun, shining and lasting difference, spreading the word, generosity, giving, presence, tenderness, listen, flexibility, stamina, relaxed, peaceful, seeking to understand before seeking to be understood, joy, trust, light sense of humor, gentleness, compassion, curiosity, patience, care, live my word, Carole, Kelsey, Jenna, Larry, Raphiella, creativity, magical moments, principles, balance, father, one million books sold*

1. **All abundance affirmations begin the same,** with four empowering words: *I intend to receive. . . .* This phrase combines the power of receiving and free choice. In *Beyond Success* I shared the idea that receiving is actually one of the highest forms of *giving*, because when we receive openly and positively, we allow others to feel the joy and fulfillment of giving. In a very real sense, your abundance affirmations are conversations with a personal, spiritual source. By stating your intention to openly receive, you are thanking your creator for abundance and for giving you the free choice to openly receive that abundance in the form of worthwhile goals, advances in character, and transformations in attitude.
2. **Your first three abundance affirmations are fueled by your keywords** from the compelling-why answers. The first of your three will focus on a personal objective (physical, emotional, mental, or spiritual), the second on a professional or financial vision, and the third will target relationships. After you've written these three and visualized them for a week or two, you may well want to write several more, again using your keyword list for reference. I work with an average of ten abundance affirmations regularly.
3. **Create your full abundance affirmations** using the following important guidelines:
    - Use emotion-charged words.
    - Be very specific.
    - State your abundance affirmations in the positive
    - Focus on what you want and will do personally, not on trying to control others.
    - Open yourself fully to the possibility of your vision daily.

On your computer, a three-by-five-inch card, or single sheet of paper, write your opening phrase—*I intend to receive*—and then complete the abundance affirmation as described above.

Next, on the same page or on the opposite side of the card, write several statements that begin with, *I know this is true because. . . .* These statements add a vibrant dimension of faith, confidence, and conviction to the affirmation. When you state, "I know this is true," you move beyond wishy-washy hopes to certainty. Every one of your sixty trillion cells participates in that feeling of certainty, filling you with unstoppable trust. In these statements, your vision has already become reality. By adding supporting "because" statements, you bring even further validity and strength to the abundance affirmation.

The word *because* is one of the most powerful words in our culture. Xerox Corporation conducted a fascinating study of the influence this word has. In the experiment, individuals were assigned to cut to the front of a long line of people waiting to use the only copy machine in a bustling office. The "line-cutters" were given three different statements to justify their need to push their way to the front. In the first case they simply said, "I have to get this copied right away." In the second case they were instructed to add a supporting "because" statement such as, "I have to get this copied right away because we only have fifteen minutes to distribute this before the board meeting begins." In the third case, the "because" statement was nonsensical. For example, "I have to get this copied right away because I have to." The researchers found that the addition of the "because" statement—even when that statement was vague as in the third case—more than doubled the acceptance level of those waiting in line. When you add your "because" statements to abundance affirmations, you add this same kind of validation and inner acceptance to your vision.

Here is an example of a powerful abundance affirmation about a professional goal that had a dynamic impact in my life. On the front of an index card I wrote:

*I **intend to receive** a tremendous acceleration in sales of* Beyond Success *beginning immediately that will lead to a top 100 listing on Amazon.com by December 31st.*

Then on the reverse side I wrote:

*I **know** this is true because*

- Beyond Success *is such a heartfelt classic of love, insight, and empowerment*
- *I have learned so much about how to promote effectively*
- *people's spirits soar from the love and hope Beyond Success provides*
- *wonderful, passionate people have joined in the acceleration*
- Beyond Success *is the ultimate family-building guide*
- *through* Beyond Success *I am sharing my joy and purpose fully*

The Appendix in the back of this book lists several more examples of my abundance affirmations to assist you as you create your own.

Step 3: Visualizing Your Abundance Affirmations— Vision Becomes Reality

The final step in the abundance-affirmation process is to quietly and joyfully visualize the statements every day. This becomes a special highlight of your day because the time you spend visualizing abundance affirmations creates a magnificent opportunity for connection with God and with the spirit and joy of your most treasured dreams and aspirations. In these moments of visualization, you become fully present with your purpose, zeroing in on becoming the kind of spouse, parent, friend, professional, and human being you truly want to be.

To visualize your abundance affirmations, read them to yourself with great passion and joyful concentration. See and feel them as truth. When I read my "I-intend-to–receive" statements, I hold the affirmation card in my left hand and open my right hand, extending my fingers completely as if I were reaching out to God. When I turn the card over, I place my closed right hand on my heart as I begin reading each "because" statement, gradually opening my fingers as if opening my heart as I complete each affirmation. The key to the visualization process is to create an atmosphere of quiet so you may fully focus. Experiment with your body position and hand movements when visualizing your abundance affirmations until you find what feels right for you.

It is important to see how the divine connection you create through abundance affirmations can affect your life. After my first book was published, I found myself face-to-face with a new challenge—promoting *Beyond Success* to book buyers throughout the United States and Canada. This was uncharted territory for me and my team, but our passion for reaching thousands with the *Beyond Success* principles was unlimited. I was told by several "experts" that I would be extremely fortunate to sell five thousand copies because the major book wholesalers and bookstores had practically no interest in single-title, first-time authors of self-published books.

My first and most important action in tackling this seemingly immense challenge was to create the preceding abundance affirmation about *Beyond Success* so I could fill my spirit with possibility rather than fear by repeating and visualizing it at least twice each day. The results have been startling. Sales of *Beyond Success* have exceeded all expectations and climbed as high as #71 on Amazon.com from over two million titles! We were amazed at the tremendous testimonials we received for the book from Stephen Covey, Ken Blanchard, Roger

Staubach, John Robbins, Harvey Mackay, Bill Walton, Mark Victor Hansen and many other remarkable people. The finest publicist in the book business, Arielle Ford, chose to accept me as a client though initially she told us she did not have room for any more customers. The cards and letters from readers have touched our hearts with joy and appreciation. I have appeared on more than two hundred radio talk shows and several television programs including *Good Morning America*, CNN's *Business Unusual*, and the *Fox on Psychology* national news segment.

One of the most striking examples of the abundance generated from this affirmation happened when, in the midst of an extremely busy week, I had failed to take the time to visualize my abundance affirmations for four or five days. Whether pure coincidence or because of more divine forces at work, during that span orders for *Beyond Success* came to a screeching halt. I began my abundance affirmation visualization again on a Friday evening. The next morning at 6:45 A.M. I received a phone call from a man named Bob Proctor. I had never met Bob, but four different friends of mine had told me about him within a one-month period and encouraged me to send him a copy of my book. They said Bob was a real champion of others and that they felt we were kindred spirits. With so many people I respected seeking to connect us, I wrote Bob a fun letter and sent him a gift copy of *Beyond Success* a couple of weeks before my little interlude of skipping my visualizations.

I had all but forgotten about Bob until the phone rang, breaking the silence of that early Saturday morning. Bob introduced himself and absolutely bubbled with enthusiasm about my book. He has been a leader in personal development for more than thirty-five years, having teamed with such legends as Earl Nightingale and Vic Conant. Most recently millions of television viewers enjoyed Bob on Oprah where he appeared to talk about his contributions to the bestseller, *The Secret*. Bob certainly catapulted my weekend off to a flying start by telling me he felt my book was the most important and powerful he had read since devouring *Think and Grow Rich* by Napoleon Hill in 1960. In fact, he had carried a copy of Hill's masterpiece with him every day since then, and said he would now start carrying *Beyond Success* as well! By the time we finished talking that morning he had ordered copies for about a hundred individuals from all over the United States and Canada who paid many thousands of dollars a year to have Bob mentor them. Within a few weeks after the call, he sent them all a powerful letter asking each of them to order at least one full case of *Beyond Success* to give to important people in their lives and to include a letter with each copy they gave encouraging the recipient to do the same thing! Suddenly we were in the midst of an amazing acceleration.

The visible results of abundance affirmations have certainly not always been as dramatic as that remarkable Saturday. At times the process is much more subtle. But when I look back over the years, the impact of these statements has been astonishing. Every aspect of my life I hold most dear, from my family to my professional pursuits to my physical, emotional, and spiritual health, has been elevated through the faith, possibility, and energy I have received from writing and visualizing these magical statements. Each moment you spend with your abundance affirmations is a precious moment of connection with divine spirit, a loving conversation with a joyful God. Abundance affirmations are tremendous vehicles to keep you on track with your true purpose and compelling why, the most constant sources of abundant energy.

Igniting Others' Energy Through Questions

As parents, friends, teachers, coaches, and businesspeople we not only want to cultivate and enhance our own energy level, but often wish to help others ignite greater energy within themselves. Your effectiveness as an "energy activator" will soar when you remember a foundational principle of true leadership: *Ask more than tell!* Questions are magical energy sparks because they inspire thought, discovery, and creativity.

In my seminars, attendees participate in multiple "interview sessions" in which they ask one another several enabling questions.

I am constantly struck by the crescendo in energy level that spreads throughout the room as the interviews progress. Faces light up and gestures become animated and vibrant as the questions catalyze discovery and spur treasured memories. The heightened energy is shared by both the interviewer and the interviewee. Often the connection becomes so strong that the participants begin to look like mirror images of each other.

Enabling Questions for Children

For parents, nothing is more important than finding ways to effectively assist their children to develop confidence and believe in themselves. No skill will be more valuable to impart than the ability to think creatively, flexibly, and innovatively. This requires that children be free to discover, to create, and to adventure. They must have the chance to explore unknown territory and the energy to find their way, even if it means taking some wrong turns and making some mistakes.

At the same time, we want to take great care of our children so they feel safe and protected. That's why, when we see a potential rough spot ahead, we so often feel compelled to *tell* rather than *ask*. And what do we tell our children? *More often than not we tell them what we don't want them to do!* After all, it appears to be so much easier and more efficient to say, "Don't do that!" than to ask, "How would you handle that?" Yet, there is an underlying paradox at work here. If I say to you, "Don't think of the number three," what happens? Immediately the number three pops into your head, and then you quickly try to push it out. The same is true when we tell our children not to spill their juice or not to forget to do their chores. When we describe what we don't want, we magnetically direct their focus toward that which we don't want! In other words, what we focus on is what we create.

A good first step in a new direction is to describe what you *do* want from and for them. Yet even this often leaves the children uninvolved, merely performing mechanically and without passion, energy, or spirit. The job may get done, but without real ownership and understanding.

For what is the long-term impact of telling rather than asking? When you constantly "tell," and describe what is to be done, what do you take away? The answer is *discovery.* Only by facilitating discovery do you enable others to become passionately involved, taking full ownership of a concept, challenge, or opportunity.

That is why often the very best choice as a parent is to ask rather than tell, particularly if you ask enabling questions such as the following:

- "How will you feel to complete all your work so well?"
- "What would be a really effective way to get this done and have fun in the process?"
- "What do you think is the best way to accomplish this?"
- "Why does your full effort make such an important difference?"

Instantly, through questions like these you invite your children to think, to feel, and to develop a purpose that has genuine meaning for them.

Enabling questions are also magnificent momentum builders for children's spirits. Here are some simple momentum-building questions to ask your children each evening before they go to sleep. (Incidentally, these same questions are equally valuable to ask yourself or any teammate you want to help build unstoppable positive anticipation about tomorrow!) I call these the *Upward Spiral Questions.*

- "What did you do today that was really great?"
- "What about that made it so terrific?"
- "How did it make you feel?"
- "What did you *give* today that made someone else feel happy?
- "How did *giving* make you feel?"
- "What did you learn today that you are excited about?"
- "What are you looking forward to tomorrow?"

As you ask this simple set of questions consistently over time, you will be delighted to watch your children begin to look ahead with positive expectancy and enthusiasm. Have you ever noticed the damaging tendency most people have to blow disappointments, confrontations, or mistakes way out of balance and proportion? Suppose that, in a given day, forty different major events occurred—meetings, telephone conversations, exercise, meals, decisions, projects, etc. Of those forty events, thirty-nine ranged from satisfactory to outstanding. But one of those forty events in the day was a real bummer—a rejection, an unpleasant confrontation, a mistake, frustration, or disappointment. What would you say most people focus on as the day comes to a close? The bummer! Do you think it might affect their sleep and even their dreams? Could it have an impact on their energy and vitality when they try to get up the next morning?

Somehow this pattern becomes conditioned in us, starting as children, as a sort of defense mechanism. On the surface it would appear to provide protection by keeping us from getting our hopes up too high. Unfortunately, expecting the worst can easily become a self-fulfilling prophecy. When we hold onto our setbacks and disappointments, we subconsciously carry that doubt and negative energy into our next endeavors and—voila!—the exact results we feared become reality.

The Upward Spiral Questions reverse this disempowering tendency to focus yourself, your associates, and your children on the negative. By asking these simple questions, you help them look forward to the opportunity inherent in tomorrow rather than the potential for failure, embarrassment, or rejection. You assist your children in believing that great things are possible when they come from a place of enthusiasm and energy. You may need to be persistent at first, because your children may not be accustomed to questions that ask them to reach into their hearts and spirits. But soon they will look forward to the questions and may even begin to ask you for your answers. In my own experience as a coach, teacher, and business executive, I have seen the phenomenal results of consistently building this upward spiral within myself and others through enabling questions. Consistently answering the Upward Spiral Questions actually toughens the spirit, because a reserve of positive expectation is ingrained that helps those we care about rapidly transform setbacks to "bounce-backs."

In my seminars I am constantly reminded of a delightful truth. Because my programs are alive with games, exercises, surprises, and fun, I have the joy of watching even the most skeptical, reserved adults loosen up and elevate their spirits. They rediscover the playfulness, vitality, and openness of their youth. As they do so, they reveal there is no barrier between childhood and adulthood, only a suspension bridge. The best part is when they discover that they, themselves, operate the control room that lowers or raises the bridge, creating connection or separation. Suddenly it becomes clear that adults can access the playfulness and enthusiasm of childhood. That's why the enabling questions for children are just as applicable and valuable for "kids of all ages." Use them with your teammates in your business, your friends, and all the people you love, and watch them soar to new heights.

Enabling Questions and Beliefs

Perhaps our most important work as human beings is to help others develop empowering, confident, and possibility-expanding beliefs. But let me ask you a question. What is a belief?

Before we define a belief, let's ask another important question. Do you have any beliefs today that are different from those you held just five years ago? Whenever I ask this question in my seminars, virtually every hand goes up. It's a simple yet revealing way to demonstrate one thing we know about beliefs—they can *change.*

So, now, let's come back to the question: What is a belief? Speaker and author Anthony Robbins offers a very simple, clear definition: A belief is nothing but a feeling of certainty about what something is or means. The strength of a belief is determined by the quantity and quality of the reference experiences that support that belief.

In other words, if we envision a belief as a stool, the seat portion is the belief itself, while the four legs upon which the seat rests represent the references. If we add even more legs (references), the stool (belief) becomes even more stable. But, if we start sawing off the legs one by one, the stool can topple. So, a goal for every leader is to help the team and every individual strengthen their enabling beliefs while replacing the disabling ones. The key question is this: how do you assist others (and yourself!) to change disabling beliefs?

Once again, the transformational tool is your set of enabling questions. First, however, you must activate your alertness and powers of observation. You must look deeply into your teammates' hearts to discover what they truly believe. Sometimes they will say they have positive belief, but their nonverbal communication—their body language—is screaming with doubt and uncertainty.

When you sense that they do not truly believe their stated goals are possible —or that they believe they lack the talent, tenacity, or resources to accomplish their desired outcomes—there are some foundational questions to help them replace weak, termite-infested "legs" with new timber, strong enough to support winning beliefs. I call these the *Transformation Questions*, because only when disabling beliefs are replaced with new enabling ones does genuine transformation become possible.

Transformation Questions

1. What have you already accomplished even though, when you began, you had no idea how you'd pull it off?
2. How did you do it?
3. How did it make you feel?
4. What did you learn from the experience?
5. How would you accomplish your present goal if you knew it was possible?
6. What would make you absolutely unshakable in your determination to successfully achieve your goals?
7. How would you achieve ten, twenty, or fifty percent of your goal?*
8. How will you feel to reach this objective?**
9. What will it mean to your team?***

* Often it is the degree of change or improvement people believe is required that is challenging. Through this question you help them move in the direction of their goal. Instantly they find themselves viewing their ultimate destination from a new, closer, more achievable perspective.

** This is a *compelling-why* question. Compelling whys give rise to breakthrough hows! When your teammates visualize the rich and positive emotions they will feel from the achievement of their goals, they will increase both their inspiration and their strategic creativity. This question also includes an enabling presupposition that the goal has already been achieved.

*** There is no single, more powerful way to intensify positive, compelling emotion than to fill your visualizations with those you care about deeply.

Every time you ask others the Upward Spiral Questions and Transformation Questions, be prepared to watch their spirits rise and energy surge. As you sense their growing faith and belief, you will be rewarded with the unmatched joy of helping others access more of their true potential. When you ignite energy in others you cannot help but elevate your own!

Chapter 5
Create a Livelihood in Concert With Your Values

Bolstered by your increased vitality and purpose from enriching your energy and identifying your compelling why, you're ready to explore new possibilities in the area of your *livelihood.* When Diana dove into a livelihood she relished, she discovered color, emotion, and energy which she used to catapult her life from a rough sketch into a true masterpiece. Like Diana, many of us want to change our livelihood paradigm because we have a passionate desire for more control of our time, our careers, and our financial present and future. When you consider that many of us spend the majority of our waking hours working, it becomes suddenly clear that deriving greater satisfaction and inspiration from our livelihood is an absolute necessity if we are to live with a truly joyful spirit. Yet so many people are unhappy and unfulfilled in their work. How can you create a livelihood that fills your spirit rather than draining it? How can you take this job and *love* it?

There are three keys to claiming a more joyful livelihood—*flexibility, personal responsibility,* and *residual income.*

Key #1: Flexibility

You'll soon see, as we journey back through the history of predominant livelihoods, that never before has flexibility been more crucial to our careers, our balance, and our economic well-being. For centuries, the dominant livelihood was agriculture. People ate the food they grew, then sold the excess for capital or bartered it for supplies. Agriculture was a self-sustaining and enduring way of life because the family farm was passed on from generation to generation. Then came the Industrial Revolution, and suddenly factories and manufacturing became the centerpiece of livelihood. Thus began the exodus from a largely rural society to an increasingly urban one.

The primary value driving both the agricultural and industrial lifestyles was *security.* Even a generation ago the standard vision of livelihood for most people centered on lifetime employment with a large corporation. The corporate career path was simple: you'd work for twenty-five to thirty-five years, retire with that shiny gold watch, and ride off into the sunset. But with the advent of a new era driven by information, services, distribution, and technology, we have experienced a dramatic paradigm shift.

Several studies have predicted that the young people of today will experience six to eight major career changes in their working lives—whether within the same company or industry or not. To adjust to this acceleration, some of the most successful and innovative corporations are reinventing not only how they do business, but often what kind of business they are in. Small businesses, especially home-based businesses, are changing even more rapidly as they become increasingly attractive alternative livelihood possibilities. In fact, we're seeing many progressive companies embracing the home-based concept and introducing new work-at-home options and completely new ways to distribute goods and information services. This explosive change is why flexibility is such an important key to creating new joy and fulfillment in your livelihood.

Flexibility stems from a hunger to learn, combined with a constantly empowering belief in possibility. But without a high level of physical, mental, emotional, and spiritual energy, it is difficult to develop and maintain flexibility. That is why it's crucial to become an energy champion first if you wish to flourish in your livelihood. Flexibility is nourished by heightened energy.

Seeking truth and alignment with your inner values enables you to take a quantum leap toward a joyful spirit by replacing debilitating ego with the unleashing power of flexibility. You can increase your flexibility by regularly asking yourself two pivotal questions. The first is, "What's my most important next step?" This question helps you prioritize your choices, awakening you to move in the direction of what you truly want. It takes you out of the past and helps you refocus on what is most important *now*.

The second question to ask is, "Are my present actions and choices working?" It's been said that the definition of insanity is doing the same thing over and over again and expecting a different result. Yet how easily do we fall into the pattern of repeating choices that create no progress? Each of us has elements in our lives that feel forced. We have to drag ourselves to complete these tasks or duties. Still others have become so routine, so devoid of passion that we perform them robotically. By asking, "Are my present actions and choices working?" we rediscover that we truly have choices. When things aren't working we can try something different.

Mahatma Gandhi was one of the most flexible thinkers in history. He constantly asked himself flexibility questions because he strongly favored change over consistency when consistency was leading to complacency and inadequate results. He noted, "At the time of writing I never think of what I have said before. My aim is not to be consistent with my previous statements on a given question, but to be consistent with truth as it may present itself to me at a given moment. The result has been that I have grown from truth to truth."

Key #2: Personal Responsibility (PR)

The second key to developing a joyful livelihood is a new kind of PR. I don't mean public relations—I mean *personal responsibility*. In *Beyond Success* I introduced the concept of HIQs, HAQs, PÍQs, and EPIQs. A HIQ is a hopelessness-inducing question such as, "Will this work?" The question becomes a HIQ when it's delivered not with curiosity or openness, but with doubt. A HAQ—a hopelessness-assured question—goes one step further. The more you live in the land of HIQ, the more likely you'll move deeper into feelings of hopelessness. You'll add superlatives to anchor your sense of doubt by asking the HAQ, "Will this *ever* work?" Both HIQs and HAQs depend upon the decision to give up personal responsibility. It's that feeling of, "I could do better, but it's my boss," or "It's the economy," or "Why do things have to change?" or "If it wasn't for everything outside of me and around me, things would be much better."

To inject far greater joy in your livelihood and your life, become a PR master instead. As soon as you embrace the gift of personal responsibility fully, you stop dwelling on things outside your control and, instead, begin to build enthusiasm about growing, developing, and changing *yourself*. You are suddenly alight with inner knowing that *who you are makes a difference*. Instead of giving up hope, you realize how important your choices are and how much they count. Individuals and companies that focus on developing personal responsibility will succeed mightily in expanding their livelihood paradigms—especially when they combine this principle with new choices in the third and fourth areas you'll learn about later in this book.

When you accept a higher level of personal responsibility, you become a *servant leader*. Your goal is to serve. A servant leader is one who leads not by position, power, or title, but through example and a complete commitment to service. When you think about the absolutely finest companies or organizations, it becomes readily apparent that the dedication to serve is a foundational ingredient in their success.

Personal responsibility is the fundamental key to the dedication to service. Through personal responsibility you move from "What's going to happen to me?" to "What can I make happen and what can I do for you?" You leave the land of HIQs and HAQs and become a PÍQ (as in "peak") player. PÍQ stands for a possibility-inducing question. Suddenly you stop putting yourself "at the effect" and exercise your choice to be a cause of hope and possibility. When you combine true team spirit with dedication to service by asking, "How will I contribute so that *we* make this work for the team?", you have created an EPIQ (pronounced "epic")—an exciting possibility-inducing question.

What do you notice about people who love to serve? When you become aware of the people you know who really love to serve, you notice that there is something very special about these folks. They're happy! They're what I call *solutionists*. For many years I embraced the statement, "It's not what happens, it's what you do that makes the difference." But people who relish the opportunity to serve take this principle a step further. In *A Simple Path*, Mother Teresa said, "It's not just what we do that makes the difference—it's the love we put into the doing." Mother Teresa's order of the Sisters of Mercy continues to manifest this magnificent principle daily. Working in utter poverty as they care for starving, disease-ravaged people, these Sisters live not in despair but in joy. Often their greatest service is simply to be there, gently sending love, as those they care for breathe their last breaths. Yet in the midst of such sadness and seeming darkness, the Sisters find peace and light because they see their work as service to God, and to the loving spirit in which God views all life.

When your goal is to serve, to bring out the best in every person and situation, you realize that both what you do and the love you put into the effort is one hundred percent up to you. "If it's to be, it's up to me!" **When your goal is to get rather than give, you deactivate your personal responsibility, leaving your happiness, inner satisfaction, and, ultimately, your peace of mind up to someone else.** In the paradigm of joyful livelihood, leadership that is driven by a dedication to serve will emerge as the only truly successful and enduring form of leadership both of self and others.

Have you ever worked with a leader who seemed far more interested in serving and developing you than in personal glory or power? How did you feel about him or her? What kind of performance and growth did it inspire when the leader focused on serving you and the customer, and demonstrated that focus through personal action and energy? Nearly two thousand years ago Jesus taught his followers the joy and peace that comes from a life dedicated to service. If the love we fail to share is the only pain we live with, those who lead through service have discovered how to live pain-free! There is no greater motivator than a leader who loves to serve.

Key #3: Residual Income

The third key to finding greater joy in your livelihood is clearly understanding and using the concept of *residual income.* Put simply, residual income is income that continues to be generated long after your initial efforts to earn it. **A foundational key to creating a truly abundant livelihood is to develop solid sources of residual income.** Three primary sources of residual income are investments, royalties, and certain forms of businesses such as franchising and network marketing or direct sales. As you begin to build these sources of residual income, you may encounter obstacles and challenges. But each source can lead to lasting financial abundance and the time-freedom that it brings.

Investments

One method for building residual income is through wise investing. By successfully investing your capital, you allow it to grow through compound interest. To take full advantage of the benefits of investing, you must increase your knowledge and create a financial plan that fits your values and goals. It doesn't hurt to be blessed with a healthy supply of good luck, as well, as we all saw all too clearly with the enormous crash of NASDAQ in the late 1990s, and more recently with the stunning volatility of the stock markets in 2008! The challenge is that building a long-term, lucrative portfolio usually requires considerable time and patience. If you want to build it fast, it almost always requires substantial capital up front and a high tolerance for risk. In other words, to build residual income quickly through investments, you almost always must *have* money to make money. But if you make the commitment to develop a financial plan you believe in with a balance of risk and security, and you stay with it, keeping an eye out for new opportunities as they arise, you'll have a solid likelihood for success. The benefits you can derive through perseverance on this path to residual income are potentially huge. The following story demonstrates the remarkable opportunities for residual income that can occur when you understand the dynamics of investing.

Once there were two wealthy, rather eccentric friends who loved to play golf together every week. They were evenly matched and just couldn't wait for each Saturday to see who would play best. To spice up the action, they thought of all kinds of extravagant wagers to place on their games. One Saturday, one of them said, "Let's put some real heat on today. If I lose, I'll pay you $18,000—$1,000 per hole." Now, the other player was shrewd and understood that wise investing builds residual income. He knew, though they were evenly matched, he almost always bested his partner on the last hole because, being a far longer driver, he found himself in a much better position to score a birdie or a par. So he casually suggested, "Okay. If I lose, I'll pay you $18,000, but I'd like to try something a little different. How about if we have another side bet today? **Just for fun, let's start with one dollar on the first hole and double the amount on each successive hole, and whoever wins the eighteenth hole will win the bet.** How does that sound?" His partner shrugged and said, "Well, okay, it doesn't seem fair that you'll have to pay me $18,000 and you're willing to take so little if you win, but it's your money. Okay, you're on!"

Sure enough, the shrewd character outscored his partner as usual on the last hole even though he lost the overall match by two shots. The winner was smiling broadly as they walked together into the clubhouse. Pretending to be disappointed and upset, the clever player wrote him a check for $18,000 right on the spot. "You sure played well; you deserve this." Then he said, "By the way, let's figure out where we ended up on my side bet. I birdied the eighteenth so at least I won our little side wager. Let's see: we started at one dollar on the first hole; the second was two dollars; that made the third hole four dollars; the fourth was eight dollars." His friend interrupted him complaining that this could take forever.

"Just cut to the chase and tell me what I owe you."

"Okay, okay. So, let's see. . . If you double a dollar eighteen times, that brings the total to . . . $131,072. But, you can just round it to $131,000. And, by the way, thanks a lot!"

His friend's jaw dropped to the floor. You see, all investing and other forms of residual income have this special capacity. If you keep building, though it may take time to gather steam, eventually it jumps dramatically. It took fifteen holes for the wager to build up to a little over $16,000. But in the last three holes the value exploded all the way to $131,000. The bottom line with investing and residual income is to stay with it.

Royalties and Franchising

The second form of residual income is royalties from a successful creative endeavor. You could write a best-selling book, become a movie or recording star, or patent a great new invention. The challenge is that relatively few of these are successful enough to earn substantial royalties. But if you've got the dream, the most important quality in developing this form of residual income is perseverance.

The third vehicle for generating residual income is participating in some form of business opportunity that builds residual income into the overall compensation package. Some of the top companies today, like Microsoft, Apple, and many others, are leading this direction within the corporate marketplace by designing lucrative stock-option plans, 401(k)s, IRAs, and other residual-income builders.

Today, however, more and more people are deciding to step out of the traditional corporate path and begin their own businesses. It's truly a livelihood revolution, fueled by accelerating technology that is inventing whole new industries and making others archaic practically overnight. What if you had been a leader in the music CD industry in the 1990s? Technology has radically changed that industry. Now iPods and media players on our personal computers have created a revolution in the way we store and listen to music. Only those who adapt to industry changes will flourish.

This is just one dramatic example of the seemingly overnight upheavals we are seeing in many people's livelihoods. But here's a provocative thought—within virtually every field there are similar technological transformations moving forward. You don't know when such radical changes may impact your industry. When you combine this technological uncertainty with the continuing workforce changes, and the fact that more than fifty percent of the Fortune 500 companies from just twenty years ago no longer exist, **the old idea of lifelong security through corporate employment needs careful reexamination.** That's why so many people are taking a close look at other options and choosing to build their own businesses, either as additional sources of income or as the central one.

One of the alternatives that shifted the livelihood paradigm for many people was franchising. The original idea behind franchising was to own your own business—your franchise—yet still receive the benefits of working with a solid, established company: the franchisor. In many cases the franchisor would provide you with a detailed "turn-key" operation so you could run your business using systems and procedures that had already been designed and proven.

Even though franchises represent a very significant portion of the global economy today, when they first hit the American scene they were viewed as such a radically different way of doing business that the franchising concept came within eleven votes of being denied by Congress as a viable, legal form of business. In fact, the idea of a business operation like McDonald's was initially considered a sort of insidious scam! Yet in the 1990s, approximately thirty-three percent of the total GNP in this country came from franchises. It's become difficult to find a single block in a typical American business district without at least one franchise. That kind of dramatic success demonstrates that new paradigms can flourish once a critical mass of people embraces the change.

Yet in recent years it's become increasingly costly and difficult to open a franchise. There are some significant challenges inherent in this form of business today, beginning with the cost of entry—an average of well over $100,000 just to get up and running. For most new franchisees the time demands are also extraordinary, with practically every minute of the day swallowed up in bringing the new business up to speed. That commitment often means little time for family, recreation, or any semblance of balance in your life. It's also an extremely regulated industry. What's more, once you get your franchise up and running, you must pay royalties to your franchisor for every dollar you bring in. **The truth is that franchises were created to produce residual income for the franchisor, not the franchisee!** And for many franchisees, the toughest obstacle may be the slow and often painful road they must travel to earn back their initial investment. You keep plowing money back into the franchise for several years before you start to see real profits. The net return is generally low, so most successful franchisees today own several franchises. This gives the franchisee more of a residual income base, but increases the complexity and time required to operate and manage several different facilities and staffs. Despite these challenges, franchising with the top companies does provide great satisfaction for many franchisees, combining the pride of owning a business with the security of a systematized, turn-key operation.

Network Marketing

Today another form of business has taken the baton from franchising and is sprinting into the forefront as a tremendous new opportunity for building residual income. It's the livelihood revolution known as home-based businesses. **One of the most powerful, sensible, and exciting forms of home-based businesses is *network marketing*.**

It's critical to understand what network marketing is and what it's not. Network marketing with a quality company is not a pyramid scheme. Those illegal and unethical games still pop up from time to time in our society, and they soil the name of network marketing, though they have absolutely nothing to do with it. You can spot a pyramid by observing that no real goods and services are bought or sold. In a pyramid scheme, you are required to make a large investment up front without receiving real goods or services. You're asked to put your money into a growing till, and once enough people are convinced to do the same thing, then you move to the top of the pyramid. Theoretically, you're supposed to receive lots of money for very little work. In reality, many people get hurt in pyramid schemes and lose their investments, while the very few who started the scheme can cash in.

Network marketing is completely different. It's ethical, viable, and as you'll see, incredibly practical. Here's why.

In network marketing with a quality company, top-notch products or services are bought and sold. Generally a very small initial investment—often less than a hundred dollars—puts you into your very own business. As a distributor in a network marketing company, you share the products, services, and business opportunity with others. You earn commissions and bonuses when you and your team ("downline" or "success line") purchase the products and services from the company for personal use or to sell to consumers. In many of the best network marketing companies there is no requirement to maintain an inventory; the people you interest in your products or services buy directly from the company.

As long as you believe deeply in the products and services a network marketing company has to offer, it's an effective, simple, and incredibly fun way to build a home-based business. **Network marketing is a leader in the new paradigm of joyful livelihood because of the choices and flexibility it offers.** For example, you can begin part-time, or you can choose to work your network marketing business as a full-time career. Network marketing is also refreshingly cooperative because you succeed by helping the people you sponsor become hugely successful. Thus, with network marketing you automatically share in the success of others, and they share in yours—it's the ultimate win-win system.

My wife, Carole, has been running a network marketing company for a few years, and it's been a fantastic addition to our lives. She works at it part-time because our number-one priority is our children and she spends a great deal of her time with them. We've been delighted with the progress she's made putting four to eight hours a week into her business. She's been able to build quite a successful home-based enterprise, adding a great extra kick to our monthly income. What's exciting about this road to residual income is that she's traveling it with friends and family and making new friends who, in turn, begin to build their residual income. And perhaps the most satisfying aspect for Carole is working with a company she deeply admires and distributing products and services she loves. Every day she feels the inner satisfaction of knowing she's making a positive difference in the quality of life for others. Her network marketing business has enabled her to grow as a servant leader.

So an important key to expand the joy in your livelihood is to take personal responsibility for generating sources of residual income. They must be sources that align with your values, and you must be flexible in your approach yet intent on your vision. By constantly focusing on creating value for others through your dedication to serve, you will discover abundance and fulfillment in your chosen livelihood.

You rapidly accelerate building a joyful spirit in your livelihood when you apply your expanded understanding of energy. And with the increased financial freedom and abundance you'll realize from a livelihood centered upon flexibility, personal responsibility, and residual income, you'll open new choices about where to focus your improved vitality. The moving story of Mark Segars and his family provides a shining example of the possibility available when you seize the opportunities generated from the combination of empowering energy and joyful livelihood.

My friend Mark is a gentle, deeply caring human being who's built a tremendously successful network marketing business featuring food supplement products that help promote energy. He is dedicated to using the products himself, so his own physical and mental vitality are exceptional. A few years ago he returned home from his company's annual gathering to some devastating news: His two-year-old daughter had been stricken with a form of childhood cancer. Immediately Mark dropped everything and for many months focused one hundred percent on finding the best possible pathway to beat the cancer and on helping his daughter become well. As a home-based business owner he was right there with his little girl throughout the day. Because of the choices he made consistently about diet and exercise, he maintained remarkable physical vitality through this difficult time, which allowed him to put his full life force and spirit into his compelling why—helping his daughter and his family. Because he had built a successful network marketing business, a number of critically important benefits supported the Segars family as they fought to save their little girl. First, his growing, thriving business was based upon residual income, which meant that even though he completely stepped away from focusing on his work for a considerable period of time while his full energy was concentrated on his family, his business continued to grow. He had been such a superb sponsor and coach with the people in his network marketing organization that they simply took the ball and kept right on going. As a result, he experienced no drop in income. Second, because his network marketing income was quite substantial, the Segars family had the financial abundance to choose whatever treatment they felt offered the greatest care and greatest hope for their daughter. Several of the treatments they chose were considered alternative and consequently not covered by medical insurance, yet Mark was able to pay for them without hesitation. All that mattered was his daughter. Finally, because a successful network marketing business is all about building a connected team, he was supported by the well wishes of thousands of people. The Segarses received countless cards, letters, and calls of support letting them know of the prayers, hope, and faith focused on their family.

Today Mark Segars' daughter is healthy and has the promise of a terrific life. Mark's choices have created a wonderful livelihood that supports family, abundance, and freedom.

We are all hungry for greater possibility for ourselves and those we love. Like the Segars family you can cultivate growing belief in possibility by seizing the opportunity inherent in each of the four areas fundamental to building a joyful spirit.

Chapter 6
The Relay Paradigm—
True Devotion to Your Team

The third area in which a fundamental shift can bring you greater inner satisfaction and happiness than you've ever imagined is especially dear to my heart. I call it the *Relay Paradigm.* **The Relay Paradigm is the manifestation of the almost magical transformation that occurs when people devote themselves to others, eagerly giving their very best for the good of the team.** To put it simply, we're seeing a dynamic shift away from the "me" generation to the "we" generation. We are now driven by a fervent desire for rich, full, and connected relationships. We want to become parts of special teams. In this new paradigm of cooperation, "ego" is being replaced by "we-go."

The Relay Paradigm has been the centerpiece of my work as a coach, teacher, and business consultant. In my years as a swim coach I marveled at this almost magical relay effect. It didn't matter what level of experience or expertise the swimmers had attained; they always elevated themselves to a higher level when participating in relays. In observing this powerful principle of teamwork, I identified three keys to becoming a master in the Relay Paradigm.

- **The first is developing absolute certainty** that whatever your team needs, you'll deliver. When you move from "wanting" to do your best to *absolute certainty*, you suddenly accept total responsibility for your contributions.
- **The second key is having a compelling purpose** that's much bigger than you are—a grand compelling why. The story of movie icon Elizabeth Taylor provides a vivid example. In the late 1980s, she was in dire physical and emotional straits. She was overweight, addicted to medications and alcohol, and perilously near death. But something happened by the early 1990s—the change in her was absolutely incredible! She looked, felt, and acted about twenty years younger. Her transformation occurred because she embraced the Relay Paradigm. She found a compelling purpose much bigger than herself, one to which she was absolutely determined to give every ounce of love and devotion. For her that purpose was leading the fight to find a cure for AIDS. She became a passionate team builder, changing virtually every aspect of her life.
- **The third key is to embrace competition,** a natural outgrowth of the first two keys to the Relay Paradigm. Once you're absolutely certain that you'll eagerly give everything you can to your team, and you've committed yourself to a purpose that extends well beyond yourself, you no longer fear competition. In fact, competitors become dynamic energy sources because they help you discover more of your own true potential. You actually want them to excel, because you know their excellence will enable you to gain more energy and concentration.

In the Relay Paradigm, competition becomes the supreme form of cooperation. I saw a magnificent example of this concept not long ago when I watched a concert video featuring two virtuoso violinists. They built greater and greater passion into their music as they gathered energy from one another. It was incredible—as one would play a stunning solo, the other listened in complete rapture, soaking in the very soul of the music. Then the other, filled with exultation, would answer, reaching into the depths of her spirit to produce a level of mastery that lifted the audience to an explosion of joy. The music kept rising and rising as they inspired even greater magnificence in one another. The magic that was created beat with the heart of the Relay Paradigm.

One of the most important changes that occurs when you become a master player in the Relay Paradigm is the way you view *differences*. In our culture, we tend to push differences away. When we speak of having differences with another person it means we are in conflict, not getting along. This cultural conditioning often leads to a position of defensiveness and distrust. Masters of the Relay

Paradigm find ways to bring people's unique perceptions, talents, ideas, and qualities together. These differences are essential keys to building a far richer whole. To honor, value, and merge differences is the underlying secret of producing synergy where one plus one can equal a hundred. If everyone saw the world just as I did, we wouldn't see very much! It is our differences that often spark fresh, creative ideas and accelerate our forward momentum. By first honoring and then working to mesh differences rather than fearing them, we dissolve one of the primary sources of unhappiness and open ourselves to joy.

Merging differences is the essence of genuine collaboration. In my seminars, we play a game that delightfully reveals that most of us have never been truly taught to collaborate. Pairs of participants are supplied with the same raw materials and asked to create the greatest number of combinations they can from the materials. After instructing the pairs that this is a game of collaboration, I give them exactly two minutes to come up with a solution.

It is fascinating to observe the way the two-person-teams tackle this challenge. Though they have been told that this is a game of collaboration, they really do very little collaborating. Usually each person works with his or her own materials individually, simply checking in every so often to see how the partner is doing. But the essence of collaboration is combining resources. If the pairs had begun by bringing their raw materials together rather than working separately, they would have exponentially increased their potential. In this game it is the difference between sixteen possible combinations when they do not combine resources, and 512 when they do! It is a vivid demonstration of the synergy we can create when we combine our different ideas and insights. We always have lots of laughter when we integrate the exercise and divulge the principle it teaches.

Let's Not Wait for a Catastrophe to Join the Relay Paradigm

Traveling by airplanes as often as I do, I'm always curious about the people who end up beside me on my journeys. I've met some fascinating people this way. Intuitively, I have a powerful sense that we were not placed together by chance. More and more I have come to view these flying partners as special gifts from God. These thoughts filled my mind as I made my way to my seat on a flight from Dallas to Salt Lake City several years ago.

The man beside me on the flight that day radiated a warmth that immediately captivated me. He was a big fellow, carrying a few extra pounds, but with the unmistakable strength and frame of a former athlete. I guessed that he was in his mid- to late-fifties. After the flight attendant completed her safety instructions, I introduced myself to him and we began what would become a remarkable conversation. By the time we touched down at our destination, we had opened our hearts and spirits to one another, connecting at a deeply meaningful level.

Colonel Jack O'Brien had served as the Chief Chaplain of the Oklahoma City Police Department for many years. On April 19, 1995, his entire world turned upside down in one devastating moment of tragedy. The bomb blast that killed 168 innocent, unsuspecting people that morning rattled far more than steel and concrete. It grabbed hearts and spirits and shook them for all they were worth, challenging their faith and hope. Eventually, when all the rubble had been cleared, when every body had been found, the decision was made to raze the remaining structure of the building, its foundational strength crippled beyond repair. But the foundational strength of the human spirit that rose out of the agony in Oklahoma City was indestructible. Built with giving, caring, and love, it continues to be the most formidable force on the planet and a shining example of the Relay Paradigm.

As I listened to Jack talk about the way his community had come together after the bombing, it became strikingly clear that the magical ingredient in the remarkable healing that had taken place was the power of giving. **Giving is the foundational secret to mastering the Relay Paradigm.** He told of one story that seemed to capture the essence of the thousands of moments of generosity and compassion that had given Oklahoma City back its hope and faith.

Within hours after the explosion, a makeshift camp of volunteers, rescue workers, family members, friends, and survivors had been assembled near the wreckage of the Federal Building. Many supplies were badly needed. The call went out for diapers and milk for the young children. The next evening an old, beat-up Chevy, the doors hung together with wire and the paint worn away to bare metal, pulled up near the camp. Two women emerged, their clothes torn and tattered with dirt and sweat caked on their arms and faces. Jack walked swiftly but warily over to meet the two rough-looking women. Though it seemed that everyone was there to help, the explosion had sent a chill of doubt and apprehension into the hearts of even the most trusting spirits. As Jack approached these two he couldn't help but wonder about their intentions.

When Jack reached them and began to listen to their story, he was brought to tears by the simple beauty of their giving spirit. Speaking in thick Oklahoma drawls, they explained the reasons that had compelled them to come. These two were no strangers to hardship and despair. They were single mothers and lived in abject poverty with little money to feed their eight children. Their home was a tiny trailer that became like an icebox when the biting winter winds blew and then an oven in the stifling heat of the Oklahoma summer. They had little education, few skills, and scarce prospects. But when they saw what had happened to all these innocent people, their hearts went out to them. As rough as life often was for them, they realized it was nothing compared to the pain felt by the families of the bomb victims. They were determined to find some way to help. So, when they heard on the radio that supplies were needed for the babies, the two sisters left their trailer before the sun came up and spent all day going from house to house, doing yard work, cleaning, ironing—whatever they could to earn money. They kept the oldest daughter home from school to watch the younger children. They had driven an hour and a half in their rickety jalopy, the backseat and trunk filled with diapers and milk, and just wanted to know where they should deliver their cargo. They said they wished they had more to give but hoped this would help in some small way.

Jack hugged them gratefully, momentarily ashamed that he had doubted their intention because of their rough exterior. In their eyes he now saw the great compassion that had inspired them to action. He was deeply moved by the realization that these two, with so little, had unselfishly given so much.

In 2001, Americans were even more deeply shaken by the tragedy of 9/11. In New York City, just as in Oklahoma City six years before, the world seemed to stop in horror. Gradually, though, we made the fundamental choice to honor those who were lost that morning by caring more for one another. Everywhere across the United States, kindness, patience, compassion, and togetherness had never been stronger than in the days, weeks, and months following those horrific events. But the most important lesson we can learn from these tragedies is that we must not wait for a catastrophe to serve one another and demonstrate what kind of teammates we can truly become.

Mother Teresa has said, "Service is love in action." The two women in Oklahoma, along with countless other caring people during two national tragedies, exemplified this simple but profound truth. They showed us that we build great teams, families, and communities not by asking what we can get, but rather what we can *give*. Genuine service, motivated not by the desire to receive credit or political gain, but rather for the simple joy of knowing you helped another human being, is the essence and foundation of the Relay Paradigm.

For me, it was the pain and shock of losing Diana that awakened my understanding that *now* is the time to express my love and thanks to the people closest to me. I wrote this book to help you avoid such sadness by taking action. When it comes to building teams and families, there is simply no time like the present. A wonderful little poem so simply and profoundly states this truth:

> The past is history,
> The future a mystery,
> The gift is now . . .
> That's why they call it *the present.*

The Greatest Team Questions

Imagine the impact when the Relay Paradigm becomes our fundamental performance paradigm. We'll live in concert with one of legendary UCLA basketball coach John Wooden's greatest core beliefs: "It's amazing what gets accomplished when no one cares who gets the credit." In the Relay Paradigm, the goal is to serve, because we view ourselves as "bringer-outers." Our passion is to help everyone recognize how important they truly are. We can adopt the Relay Paradigm into our hearts right now by making the simple decision to live as a full-out team player. It is a decision that adds immeasurable richness to your life and everyone you touch.

A very powerful and connecting way to identify the essential elements in the kind of team that constantly inspires you is to sit down together with a teammate or family member and ask each other the *Greatest Team Questions.* Seek to become fully associated to the exercise by vividly imagining yourself with the team you identify. Visualize the people, hear their voices, and feel your full emotions as if you were actually with them. Each of you should spend a good three to five minutes asking and answering each of the following questions.

Greatest Team Questions

1. What was (is) the greatest team you've ever been a part of?
2. What made (makes) it such a great team?
3. How did (do) you feel to be a part of that team?

4. What did (do) you contribute to that team?
5. What did (do) you receive from that team?
6. In a phrase or sentence, how would you describe the team's mindset?
7. Where did (does) that mindset come from?

Once you've finished interviewing one another, write down the insights you've discovered from the exercise. As you write these thoughts you will be describing the actions, attitudes, and feelings that create a truly satisfying team environment for you. The questions also ignite recognition of a very empowering belief—that the team begins with you. Your decisions, contributions, and actions are the elements you directly control which have a tremendous impact on the quality of your teams. With this fresh understanding, you will be able to inject your teams with the transformative energy of the Relay Paradigm.

The Miracle of the Relay Paradigm

Years ago I conducted a seminar entitled "The Winner's Mindset" in Montreal, Canada. The final event in the seminar is called the Board Breaking Relay. It is a tremendously powerful experience of teamwork. In the exercise, participants learn to break through one-inch-thick wooden boards karate-style, as a metaphor for breaking through obstacles, fears, or limits that are holding them back in their lives. We prepare the participants by asking them to create a deeply personal meaning for the breakthrough experience. For example, someone may choose to break through shyness or self-doubt, or to shatter a limiting habit such as smoking or procrastination. The goal is to use the event as a catalyst to transform relationships, situations, or disempowering beliefs that have caused them pain, frustration, or anger. As the participants explode through their boards they access a level of energy and focus that awakens new possibility. The breakthrough becomes a dynamic symbol of their capacity to build greater joy, confidence, and belief within themselves through decision, vision, and action.

As each individual steps forward into the circle to break through, the entire team cheers uproariously, filling the room with unconditional support. In Montreal that day there were about 140 people present. As the last person stepped into the circle, the energy was absolutely soaring. Fresh with the glow of their own breakthroughs, 139 participants clapped and cheered as the final board breaker, a young woman named Anik, stepped into the circle. I waited in the center, ready to hold her board. Watching her closely as she made her way to me, I searched for signs of her state of mind. Was she nervous, fearful, confident, or intense? As Anik reached me and handed me her board, her teammates closed in around us, chanting, "Anik, Anik, Anik!" with unbridled enthusiasm. She radiated a delightful smile and twinkling eyes that let me know her complete determination to break through. She weighed at most ninety pounds, a lovely, petite young woman inspired to step beyond something immense that was holding her back in her life.

As she attempted to practice the techniques she had just learned, I could see her balance was way off. She teetered and wobbled with very little control of her body. I learned later that Anik had multiple sclerosis, which affected her nervous system and equilibrium. But despite her physical challenge, it was clear nothing was going to keep her from an all-out effort. The cheering rose to a crescendo again. Anik was ready.

But as she took aim and sought to shoot her hand forward and explode through the board, she missed it by almost two feet, her arm flying wildly off to the side, completely out of control. Then something magical happened. The team became a relay, completely devoted to supporting Anik with unstoppable enthusiasm. They lifted her higher and higher through the loving force of their spirit. **She was already a champion in their eyes because her effort was so utterly pure.** As she stepped into the circle again, their unwavering spirit seemed to help stabilize her, and she actually touched the board. But her balance was still so askew that though she managed to strike the board, it was as if she had bounced into a brick wall. She nearly toppled over backward—

but 139 people were there to catch her, refusing to let her fall. As they lifted her back to her feet, this relay team empowered Anik with a level of belief she had never before experienced. Fueled by her own determination and inspired by her team, she stepped back into the circle. Again and again she tried, edging closer and closer to her goal as she discovered new balance and strength.

All at once on her seventh or eighth attempt she burst through the board, splitting it in two like dynamite opening a mountain! Instantly we all swept her up in a gigantic, unrestrained group embrace. I burst into tears of joy along with virtually everyone else, overcome with the emotion of this sublime moment. It was incredible. Everyone was more than thrilled because, in a very real sense, when Anik broke through, every single person present did, too. That is the magic of the Relay Paradigm: Human beings have the remarkable capacity to do more and feel more for others than we would ever do and feel for ourselves. It is in this spirit that we begin to recognize that at a foundational level we are all one team.

A few days later I received a call from the man who had invited Anik to the seminar. Anik had told him that in the seconds leading to her breakthrough as her teammates roared their support, for the first time in her life she knew what it felt like to be unconditionally loved. And in that magical moment when every ounce of her mind, body, and spirit jelled into more strength and clarity than she had ever imagined, she discovered how it felt to be unconditionally loving. That is the secret of the Relay Paradigm—unconditional love, consideration, and support for others—essential elements of a joyful spirit.

Chapter 7
Opening the Window of Opportunity

The choices you've made to create greater joy and possibility in your life by shifting your energy, livelihood, and Relay Paradigm lead naturally to the *Window of Opportunity (WOO) paradigm*. It is built from the lessons of the first three paradigms, because it requires the unstoppable vitality of expanded energy; the flexibility, service, personal responsibility, and financial abundance of the joyful livelihood; and the commitment to team, collaboration, and honoring differences of the Relay Paradigm. When you combine these gifts of energy and livelihood with the essence of the Relay Paradigm (devotion to the team called humanity of which we are all a part), you have the opportunity to truly make a contribution to a better world. The WOO paradigm represents a rapidly accelerating cultural movement away from merely making a living to a fundamental desire to make a profound difference.

When the Dalai Lama won the Nobel Prize for peace, he issued a collective wake-up call by describing us as the "pivotal generation." He meant that our generation is the first in history facing the absolute necessity of making some foundational global changes, such as seriously addressing climate change and pollution if humanity is to thrive in the future. His message was one of hope, because we are also the first generation with the resources to successfully tackle this massive challenge. After listening to the Dalai Lama's acceptance speech, I began using the term "WOO" (Window of Opportunity) in my presentations to describe the narrowing opening we have before us, a passageway to discovering how to live in peace with one another and support balance and harmony on our planet.

Acting on the Future Today

Let's examine just a few of the many interrelated reasons why the WOO Paradigm is so vitally important. The first concerns the world's explosive population growth. At the birth of Christ, there were about six hundred million people on earth. It took nineteen hundred years for the earth's population to double to 1.2 billion. In the next fifty-five years, from 1900 to 1955, the world's population doubled again to 2.4 billion. It then took only thirty years to double once more. By 1985, the world's population stood at just about five billion people. We will likely number ten billion before the year 2020.

That kind of geometric growth rate creates massive new challenges facing each of us on every corner of the globe. Imagine if over the course of fifty years the number of people living in your house or apartment doubled three times! For example, four people live in my family's house. If that number were to double three times we would find thirty-two people crammed into a space meant for four. Our collective home—the earth—is experiencing just such a rapidly increasing burden. We must find long-term solutions to the problems of climate change (which author Thomas Friedman has aptly called "global weirding") from greenhouse gases, polluted air and water, a precipitous rise in degenerative diseases, and seriously depleted and demineralized soils that don't give our plants the resources they require to supply us with the nutrition we need. Homelessness, poverty, hunger, and the threat of extinction for thousands of plant and animal species affect us all. More than ever it is clear that everyone and everything on our world is completely connected.

Perhaps even more critical is our need to replace selfishness with giving, fear with consideration, and violence with kindness. On this subject, Jesus offered, "Whatever you did for one of the least of these brothers of mine, you did for me." His words have always been true, but we are just beginning to understand the depth of their importance to our survival. We have reached the point where we must recognize we are all one family called humanity. The old paradigms must change, because now either we all win or we all lose. We have a narrowing window of opportunity to turn the tide and to bring balance and harmony back to our precious planet.

One of the most exciting and inspiring movements afoot in our culture today is the intensified focus on volunteerism. Breaking free from political maneuvering, partisanship, and ego, the volunteer movement is involving more people around the world than ever before. This movement holds the greatest promise in history of uniting races and creeds, aligning the experience of the elderly with the energy and potential of youth, and re-igniting purpose for millions by sharing wisdom rather than building mistrust.

The city of Cleveland, Ohio shows how we can seize the Window of Opportunity and revitalize our communities and spirits. Only a short time ago, it was considered one of the dirtiest, most unsafe major cities in America, infamous for its polluted Cuyahoga River that caught on fire several times before the oil and debris were cleared from the water flow. Today, Cleveland is a tremendous example of possibility. The city streets in the heart of the downtown district are sparkling clean. You can feel the new spirit that has replaced resigned disillusionment with optimism in the people of Cleveland, from civic and business leaders to the folks who park your car or help you check into your hotel.

How was this astonishing transformation accomplished? The community came together with a determination to set aside differences of race, creed, and socio-economic standing and to roll-up their sleeves together to create a home that is safe, clean, and a source of constant pride for themselves and their children. Filled with the vitality born from a dedication to service and volunteerism, the people of Cleveland seized the WOO and became an example for us all.

Participating with energy, love, and team spirit in the Window of Opportunity Paradigm is our hope for the future. Individually we may be many, but together we're much. When we unite with a passionate focus on contribution, we become an unstoppable force of hope. We become dynamic paradigm shifters when we all do our part to conserve and contribute and find great joy, inner satisfaction, and peace of mind in the process.

Here is a list of practical, powerful ways you can help open the WOO for our world.[1]

1. Help stop the destruction of old growth forests, including the tropical rainforests.
2. Help clean our polluted water, air, and land.
3. Support organic agriculture.
4. Eat more vegetables, grains, and fruit, and eat less meat.
5. Educate our children in new and powerful ways. Ask them more enabling questions. Teach them to be possibility-oriented and help them discover their unique opportunities.
6. Plant trees, shrubs, and flowers to hold what topsoil we have left and reduce carbon dioxide levels in our atmosphere.
7. Reverse the ratio of criticism to praise (thirty-five criticisms to every one praise) in our culture.
8. Elevate your personal level of energy by one full point on your E-meter.
9. Campaign against addictive substances.
10. Create teams to serve the poor and destitute.
11. Clean up the inner cities so that cleanliness and order are things that can be experienced by everyone.
12. Create shelters for the homeless and teach them to help themselves.

---

1 My thanks to Daryl Kollman for many of the ideas in this important list.

13. Support recycling centers in your community.
14. Jump in and become involved in your school system—whether you have school-age children or not. All children are our children.
15. Promote diversity in culture, attitude, belief, nationality, and religion. Through differences we can create a richer whole.
16. Drastically reduce the consumption of fossil fuels.
17. Reduce our waste stream to a trickle. There is no place to put waste, and it's both expensive and potentially damaging to our environment.
18. Clean up existing toxic waste sites.
19. Support alternative health care and work to be sure it's affordable and available to everyone.
20. Reduce the flow of toxic chemicals into our environment by changing agricultural, business, and military practices.
21. Clean up our rivers, oceans, and lakes. Make them safe and beautiful so our children will want to play in them.
22. Support your favorite charity with your time and your money.
23. Sharply reduce the amount of television you watch. Use that time to connect with others, to take action, and to live your compelling why.
24. Participate in anonymous giving several times each year.
25. Grow a garden at your home, or participate in a community cooperative garden.
26. Support the arts so our children learn to appreciate and value creativity and imagination.

Seize the WOO by Being Present

When the Dalai Lama spoke of the Window of Opportunity, his focus was global. For many, though, the challenges we must address to permanently open that global WOO seem so complex and enormous we don't know where to begin to make a difference. Many of us direct our focus on the past or the future and completely miss the present.

But there is a WOO we may seize at any moment. That WOO is *now*! Every precious moment is a WOO. Indeed, when Woody Allen joked that eighty percent of success is simply showing up, he spoke with great wisdom.

Over the years, many studies have been conducted to discover what we want most from leaders. The studies have consistently arrived at the same conclusion. We want to *trust* our leaders first and foremost. As much as we want to receive respect, appreciation, acknowledgment, and a sense of importance, we must first trust that we are being treated with honesty and integrity. Without trust we feel manipulated and used. Yet the studies have never dealt with the next, pivotal question: How do leaders—whether parents, teachers, business or government leaders, or the leader within each of us—build trust at a foundational level?

The answer comes from seizing the WOO when we are with others by *being present*. Being present means that one hundred percent of your mind, body, and spirit are actually here in the present moment. Being present sends an unmistakable message at the subconscious level. In our moments of being fully present with and for others, we convey to them that they are truly *important*. When others are present for us, we feel connected, cared for, and appreciated. It is the simplest yet most powerful way we both give and receive love. Despite the impact being present has on our relationships, we often find it easier to be present for a task, project, or thing, rather than for the people with whom we are the closest.

As they so often did when they were growing up, my two daughters, Kelsey and Jenna, became my coaches, teaching me this crucial lesson about the unmatched importance of seizing the WOO to be present for the most precious people in my life.

At the time I had become so heavily involved in consulting for a company that had experienced explosive growth, I found myself incessantly on the phone, checking voice mail or e-mail, trying to iron out a seemingly endless barrage of challenges and concerns.

Night after night as my daughters prepared for bed, I'd stop off in my office for "just a moment" before reading them a story and tucking them in. The next thing I knew, I found myself submerged in twenty-five to thirty new messages even though I had cleared my inbox less than three hours earlier. By the time I finished answering the messages, my only connection with my little girls was a silent kiss long after they were sound asleep. My wife had read to them, cuddled them, and told them how much their mommy and daddy loved them.

One evening after many weeks of this, Kelsey and Jenna managed to steal a rare moment between my phone calls. They waited patiently in my office doorway until I hung up the phone, and then ran over to tell me how much they loved me. I picked them both up onto my lap, hugging them closely and relishing the unexpected moment.

After a couple of tickles and giggles, Kelsey looked up into my eyes and said, "Daddy, we miss you."

I responded, "Honey, I'm right here. I haven't been on a trip in a couple of weeks."

"I know, Daddy. I meant we miss you because it seems like you have more time for voice mail than you do for us."

Her words, so innocently and honestly spoken, shot through me, shaking me to my very soul. I had become so accustomed to being busy, so focused on keeping ahead of my inbox that I had stopped being present for my children. All at once Kelsey helped me see that in our moments of fully present connection we do more to help those we love build confidence, faith, and self-esteem than we ever will through any self-improvement technique or communication skill.

Can you tell whether or not someone is truly present? Do you know even over the phone if the person on the other end of the line is actually there in spirit as well as body? How long does it take? When I ask these questions of the participants in my seminars, the answers become immediately obvious: We simply cannot fake being present. The power of being present is unparalleled because it is not a technique.

It is a decision, one that can create immense breathroughs in your most important relationships.

After a seminar I conducted in British Columbia, I received a letter that demonstrated the immeasurable impact of the decision to be more fully present. On the last two pages of the seminar workbook, I included a plan that gave participants a series of actions they could take to bring the seminar principles into their lives. One of the most valuable actions would be for each person to choose someone to whom they commit to be more present for thirty days. This did not mean they needed to spend more time with them. It simply meant the time they did spend would be more focused, connected, and truly present.

During the seminar, a woman had been humbled by the realization of how seldom she was actually present for her five-year-old son. Determinedly, she made the commitment to become far more present than she had ever been for him. Their relationship was courteous but not warm and joyful, with a distance that left them both feeling empty. Never had her son wrapped his arms around her and told her he loved her. They coexisted rather than connected.

On the fifth day of concentrated effort at being more present with her son—five full days of taking time to play with him, setting aside the newspaper or mail and really talking with him, asking questions about his thoughts and feelings and truly listening to his answers—she was in the kitchen preparing his breakfast. He walked in as usual, but instead of sitting down to eat, he rushed over to her and embraced her with more affection than she had ever felt from him. Looking up into her eyes he smiled broadly and said, "I love you, Mommy! You're the best!" She was overcome with joy at the breakthrough in their relationship.

How often does your response to family, friends, or co-workers begin with "just a minute," "in a second," or "what"? Do you find yourself asking those around you to repeat themselves because you missed their first attempt to communicate with you? When your children or teammates seek your attention, do you often view them as interruptions rather than feeling delight at the opportunity to share some precious moments? These questions can help you to become clear about your level of presence. If you find yourself falling into any of these patterns, it's an important sign that your focus is drifting away from the present into the past or future. It's time to listen completely before formulating your responses, to turn up your tremendous powers of observation, and to seek to understand others with great heart, compassion, and unselfishness. As you do you will find your impact on others deepening and your enjoyment of life becoming richer by the moment.

Become a World-Class Buddy-Thanker

As we become more and more dedicated to being fully present, it is natural for us to seize more opportunities to appreciate and acknowledge those around us. We become world-class "buddy-thankers!" In my seminars and presentations, I often ask participants a question that awakens awareness of a pernicious habit: "Who are the people in our lives we tend to forget to thank the most?"

This question has an amazing effect because instantly almost everyone realizes that the people we most often forget to thank are those we love the most. We fall into the habit of taking them for granted. It becomes a pattern and a routine to assume they know how we feel. "Hey, I told him I loved him back in sixty-six. What does he want, mush?"

Another question enables us to examine the true consequences of this pattern of taking our loved ones for granted. The question is, does this work? The deeper we look, the more clear the answer becomes—taking one another for granted *does not work.*

When we are fresh in the glow of a new friendship, before we fall into the pattern of taking others for granted, our relationships are like magnificent hot-air balloons: full, light, colorful, and energized. But each time we forget to express the beauty we see in one another or the gratitude we feel, it's as if a thin needle is pressed into the balloon. It doesn't explode all at once, but surely and gradually, as more and more needles are added, the balloon begins to collapse from hundreds of tiny leaks. This is very much the way relationships can begin to collapse. As we fall into the habit of failing to acknowledge and appreciate others, we see joy, vitality, and connection replaced by indifference and empty coexistence.

How can we break the pattern and take an enormous leap in the direction of vibrant, fulfilling relationships? We can make the conscious decision to become world-class buddy-thankers. In the vintage Steven Spielberg movie, *Always*, the power of this simple principle was beautifully revealed. The story centers around an ace fire-fighting pilot played by Richard Dreyfuss. He is fearless behind the controls of his plane, but completely terrified when it comes to openly expressing his feelings for the woman he loves, played by Holly Hunter. Time after time he sputters and stalls as he tries to find the nerve to tell her he loves her and wants to spend eternity with her. When a terrible fire traps a team of fire fighters, Dreyfuss defies his orders to stay grounded and attempts to rescue them. Diving perilously close to the ground with winds whipping and tossing his craft like a rag doll, he miraculously manages to drop his fire retardant, opening a seam in the inferno through which the men escape. With every ounce of his skill, he tries desperately to pull his plane up to safety, but he has pressed the limit too far. He cannot clear the tall trees and he crashes, perishing as the plane goes down in a terrible explosion.

But Dreyfuss has left his most important responsibility on earth undone: He has failed to give the greatest gift—the pure expression of his love—and is left wandering around lost and suspended instead of going straight up to heaven. Suddenly he meets a lovely angel all dressed in white and portrayed by Audrey Hepburn. (Ironically, this proved to be Miss Hepburn's final performance before her death.) With elegance and compassion, the angel explains what has happened to Dreyfuss and why he has been suspended rather than sent on to a heavenly eternity. She says simply, "The love we fail to share is the only pain we leave with." Before he can move on he must complete the loving purpose for which he lived.

As I sat captivated in the theater watching this scene for the first time, the simple statement of the angel grabbed my heart and soul and shook me. I couldn't get the words out of my mind—"The love we fail to share is the only pain we leave with." I have known so many people who left this life in pain because they failed to express their love and appreciation before it was too late. I know of even more who *live* with massive pain in every moment because they cannot bring themselves to express their true feelings before someone who means so much to them passes from their lives, just as I had when I learned of Diana's passing. They never create the magical moment of connection that was meant to be, and it becomes a festering wound that never heals. As I thought more and more about the angel's words, it struck me that there is an even greater truth that opens the window of possibility and hope. By changing one word in the angel's statement, we can put ourselves at the cause rather than the effect. When we understand at our very core that *the love we fail to share is the only pain we* live *with*, we create the choice to live pain-free.

Look around at the people in your life who have made a genuine difference for you. Now *seize the WOO!* Use your creativity and imagination, but most of all your heart, to let them know all they mean to you. Become a world-class buddy-thanker. At first, you'll feel a sense of completion knowing you've given one of the greatest gifts possible to someone you care about deeply. Gradually you will come to realize that you have received every bit as much as you have given. Your relationships will soar once again, revitalized with energy, meaning, and joy.

One of the most powerful ways to become a world-class buddy-thanker and support the growth of confidence and belief in others is to simply give them the ball—to trust them to make their own choices and handle their own challenges without seeking to control them. This is an unspoken form of an enabling question that asks, "How will you make this happen?" using actions rather than words to instill confidence within them at the subconscious level. By giving others the opportunity to carry an activity or idea forward in their own way, we breathe great faith into their spirits while immediately challenging them to become fully associated, creative, and solution-oriented. We not only put them in the game, we let them know it is *their* game.

Years ago I heard a marvelous story about the tremendous enabling power of giving the ball. An experimental weekend camp had been set up for physically and mentally disabled children at a rustic retreat center in the woods of the Pacific Northwest. The concept behind the camp was to bring these children together and give them each the responsibility for some important tasks, either to help prepare and serve meals, clean the dorms and meeting areas, or set up all the necessary equipment and materials for the meetings. It was a chance to break the patterns of dependence and learned helplessness, since normally these kids were not given the opportunity to do these things for themselves. They were terribly slow and inefficient at daily tasks and lived under constant care. They had grown increasingly dependent upon others for help with even the most basic activities such as getting dressed, eating, and bathing. By the end of the weekend retreat, the creators of this breakthrough program hoped the children would discover a new level of self-worth and hope, by successfully doing far more than they previously had been conditioned to believe they could.

On the last night of the retreat, the kids joined with the counselors in preparing a special celebration with a turkey dinner. They had set the table, mashed the potatoes, decorated the dining area, and dressed themselves for the big evening. The table was spread with heaping bowls of delicious food that, for the first time in most of their lives, these children had personally prepared. It was truly a triumph of spirit. All that remained was for the turkey itself to be carried into the dining room. The children could hardly wait!

Without really thinking, the head counselor set the prize bird on a great serving platter being held by one of the smallest children. This tiny girl was severely palsied with very little control of her balance and dexterity. Practically buckling under the weight of the turkey, she nevertheless held the platter firmly and began wobbling and teetering her way toward the dining area. For one uncertain instant the counselor stood frozen, gasping as he realized the little girl could not possibly make the long trek into the dining area successfully. Automatically he began to move toward the child to rescue her—and dinner. But, just as he was about to reach her, he stopped suddenly as he looked ahead into the dining room at all the other children staring wide-eyed at their tiny teammate inching forward with the huge turkey. All the children seemed to be with her, sending her their complete support, love, and belief through their smiles and almost electrical attention. She was so completely intent upon her duty that she hadn't even noticed the counselor speeding up behind her. All that mattered to her was bringing the turkey to the table.

She kept edging forward, almost losing control of the massive platter many times. Once she nearly toppled over but managed to right herself as she leaned against the wall and regained her balance. Finally, after what seemed like an eternity, she wobbled into the great dining room. As she safely set the turkey down on the table, all the children let out a roar of approval, applauding joyously at her incredible accomplishment. The counselor stood stunned, tears streaming down his cheeks, crying and laughing at the same time. In that moment he discovered the ultimate reward that comes from the gift of allowing others to take risks that help them discover their true potential. He realized how close he had come to taking away the turkey, and with it the little girl's chance to embrace a greater spectrum of possibility for herself. But instead, he had not only created a breakthrough moment for that little child, but also for every other person present that day—including himself.

Giving is the magic fuel of the WOO Paradigm. When you reach out to give by being fully present, by expressing your feelings of love and appreciation, or simply by giving someone the ball, you open yourself to receiving true abundance. It is the abundance that comes from believing in possibilities rather than limits, in faith rather than fear. As a giver of the greatest gifts, you will discover and radiate this abundance in the form of purpose, passion, and peace.

The Magical Power of Surprise

My wife, Carole, still takes my breath away. How could she possibly look so young and beautiful? Though we've been married more than twenty years, I'm still stunned at how beautiful she is to me. As I look at my radiant wife, I know I am the luckiest man on the face of the earth. Yet there have been times through the years when Carole just couldn't see the incredible person she truly is and the profound impact she has had on so many. At these times of shaken confidence, she has doubted whether she really mattered at all.

So when the big milestone of her fiftieth birthday came into view, I knew I wanted to create a moment for Carole she would never forget--a moment that would express far more eloquently than words how deeply she is loved and appreciated.

Moments often become cornerstones in our lives that leave indelible imprints of fresh possibility, faith, connection, and transformation. In special moments, we take real steps toward understanding, connection, and confidence. When moments are amplified by the wonder of *surprise*, their impact can empower us to break through fears and doubts and to see our true possibilities. It's one of the least understood yet most powerful tools you can use as a world-class buddy-thanker.

As I thought about Carole's big day, I knew I wanted her to experience a moment that was all of these things and more. A moment she could carry always in her spirit, one that would lift her when disappointment, self-doubt, or stress challenged her peace of mind. I wanted to see her broadest smile, happiest tears, and most amazed expression of utter surprise.

It was with this compelling vision that the seed of Carole's magical moment was planted nearly a year before it would come into full bloom.

In January, I flew to New York City for a speaking engagement and a visit with my publisher. As I floated above the Eastern Seaboard, thumbing absent-mindedly through the Delta Sky magazine, I chanced upon an article about the Broadway stage version of Disney's *The Lion King.* The description and photos of the play were sensational, and it struck me that a fantastic gift for my wife would be to fly with our daughters Kelsey and Jenna (at the time, aged fourteen and eight, respectively) to Manhattan to celebrate Carole's fiftieth in style by attending the show. It would be such fun to surprise them all with the trip, and I envisioned their wide-eyed delight as we tasted the Big Apple together. But as I began to ponder the intricate, covert planning needed to pull off this caper, I began to think more deeply about Carole and what was truly most important to her in her life.

It was then that the light bulb went off for me. If this was truly to be an event of a lifetime for Carole, it had to be built around what *she* most valued and treasured, rather than what I would like the most. I had no doubt she would thoroughly enjoy *The Lion King*, and even get a big kick out of the surprise trip to New York for her birthday weekend. But something would be missing. It would be off the mark, because I would have failed to ask the most crucial questions needed to create a masterpiece moment of the magnitude I wanted her to receive. I hadn't asked, "What would *Carole's* dream of the perfect celebration look like? What means the most to her?"

Wham! The instant these questions popped into my mind, it hit me like a lightning bolt. Carole's greatest passion is for her friends and family. New York was nice, and Broadway exciting, but without sharing her fiftieth with the people she loves so dearly, it would be just another birthday and another trip. Instantly I knew that the heart and soul of Carole's celebration would be a totally different surprise than I had originally envisioned. We would *still* fly to New York City for her birthday weekend. We would *still* go see *The Lion King*. But when we arrived in the city, she would be met somewhere totally unexpected by the friends and family that have filled her life with love. All at once I knew the real reason I had accumulated my zillion frequent flyer miles as a professional speaker. It was all for Carole's moment. I would fly her friends in for one "gala gig" in Gotham. I was so inspired I wanted to jump out of that plane and get right to it.

Later that afternoon, I waited for more than an hour outside *The Lion King* ticket office. When I finally made it to the window I knew there was more than Disney magic in the air.

There was no block of four seats available for *The Lion King* until March of 2001—five months after Carole's birthday—*except* for the Sunday matinee on November 12th, the very weekend I had planned! I snatched those seats up in a flash, high-fiving the people behind me as I left the box office in triumph.

I'm a bit embarrassed to admit that in the past I have been known to get so excited about surprises that I have occasionally spilled the beans in advance of the event. That's why I decided to devise a decoy plan to throw Carole completely off track. I figured the best way to keep such an enormous surprise from my clever wife was to let her think she already knew it.

So when I arrived home from New York City I "accidentally" left *The Lion King* tickets out on the kitchen counter where I knew she'd run across them. When she found them and pressed me for an explanation, I crumbled. With feigned exasperation, I fessed up about my plan to fly her and the girls up to New York for the show. Steven Spielberg would have been proud of my acting performance as I carried on about what an ignoramus I was to have left those tickets out.

"At least," I moaned, "we can still surprise the girls."

Carole bought the act lock, stock, and barrel. After all, it was so like me to botch the surprise. Now she was my partner in the caper, completely desensitized to anything but keeping the plan from Kelsey and Jenna. This was really getting good.

During the five months leading up to November 11, I set to work arranging for Carole's closest friends from throughout her life to meet us in New York. All of my calls were made when I was on the road for my seminars. Since my daughters were also going to be surprised, I couldn't take any chances. Any communication to me from our friends had to be sent via e-mail, because Carole and the girls never checked my messages.

As soon as I began making calls, I was completely awed by the response of Carole's friends to the plan. Without hesitation, every one of them jumped in with unfettered enthusiasm. One special friend was extremely frightened of flying and would have to travel all the way from Seattle. But no matter—she would fight her fear for this event. She was coming! One of Carole's sisters had never been in a plane before—but for this celebration she'd have parachuted from the Space Shuttle.

Our wonderful friends, Robert and Kristie Werz, were the most amazing of all. They were the only participants who lived in the New York City area—out on Long Island in the lovely little haven of Seacliff. Though I was able to use frequent flyer miles for about half of the guests, the cost of flying in so many people was still pretty steep, so I asked if some of the friends coming in could stay with the Werzes at their home. Their answer stunned me.

They said, "No, *some* of the guests will not do. *All* of your friends are welcome at our home. We don't have tons of space, but it will be fun!"

These remarkable people opened their hearts and their home to seventeen travelers, most of whom they had never met. The common bond was the love they all shared for Carole—and that was more than enough.

We were to fly to New York on Saturday, and as the whole plan developed, it became clear that I needed to get everyone else there on Friday because of the varying travel schedules. After a seemingly endless stream of phone calls, arranging, re-arranging, and finalizing, all the travel itineraries were set. Robert and Kristie were primed for their roles as innkeepers and had contacted everyone by e-mail with directions and words of welcome. Virtually every square foot of floor space would be occupied by their new friends in sleeping bags and blankets. It was the grown-ups' turn for a slumber party.

With travel plans set, I turned my attention to the surprise party itself. Carole adores fine East Indian cuisine, and thanks to some great help from Kristie and the technological magic of the Internet, I was able to find the perfect restaurant, the Bukaru Grill. Not only was its menu superb, but they offered a separate banquet room ideal for a party our size. I explained the whole plan to Raja, the restaurant manager, and he enthusiastically promised to take great care of us. The vision was becoming more of a reality by the minute.

When you immerse yourself in the creation of a magical moment inspired by the power of love, great synergy is activated. I had only visualized bringing Carole's friends together for a joyful surprise and magnificent meal. But when these imaginative and likewise inspired friends found themselves together at the Werzes' home before the party, creative sparks flew fast and furious.

One of Carole's closest friends, Muff, had quite a history of orchestrating special parties for friends' birthdays and anniversaries. These fantasy events ranged from a *Great Gatsby* Gala, to a sixties-style senior prom à la the Broadway show *Grease*, to an Ethiopian tribal celebration. Each theme was chosen to fit a special interest or passion of the person whose day was being celebrated. The formula for these events always included costumes and full-out role playing. Carole had participated in many of these parties during the years she and Muff were housemates in Alaska. In fact, she had co-planned many of the events and treasured those memories filled with delight and imagination.

Carole's fiftieth gave Muff the perfect opportunity to bring her fantasy experience out of storage with a group of people charged up with energy and enthusiasm. This was to be no standard birthday party.

Everything was arranged for our friends to meet Carole, Kelsey, Jenna, and me at the Bukaru Grill at 4:30 on Saturday afternoon. Carole knew only that we were arriving in Newark at 2:30 P.M. and would surprise the girls by taking them to *The Lion King* at 1:00 P.M. on Sunday.

A few weeks before the trip, Carole had been disappointed when I told her that the Werzes were going to be out of town at a trade show the weekend we were coming to New York. We would miss them by a day. I told her I'd find a hotel in Mid-town so we would be close to the theater and shopping. After she called the Werzes and they confirmed my story, she didn't give it another thought.

On Friday, Carole and I packed bags for the girls while they were at school. When they came home that afternoon, I told them that I was going to take Carole shopping while they were at dance practice on

Saturday morning. I added that we'd have to leave a little early Saturday to swing by the airport because one of my bags had been misrouted from my trip earlier that week and had finally come in. It was not at all unusual for my bags to arrive late, so Kelsey and Jenna were oblivious to any trickery. Carole was thoroughly enjoying the entire thing.

Late Friday night as Carole unwound in a hot bath, I snuck downstairs to check my e-mail one last time before the big day. Sure enough, there was a message from Kristie posted less than a half-hour before. The message practically jumped off the screen in delight. Kristie bubbled about how much fun everyone was having making plans together, and that they had come up with something terrific.

I was to tell Carole that I had been surfing the net for cool things to do in New York City and had found something she'd really enjoy. It was the hottest thing in the Apple—a new traveling dinner theater group called "The Way Off Broadway Players." They would be performing at a five-star Indian restaurant, the Bukaru Grill, on Saturday evening. We needed to arrive by 4:30 because the first show was to begin at 4:45. The second show was already sold out. Kristie ended the e-mail by telling me this was going to be better than anyone could have imagined. I didn't know what all they were up to, but with that kind of synergy and exuberance, I couldn't wait to find out.

That night was less a time of rest for me than of bubbling anticipation. In fact, this waiting was the toughest part of the entire escapade, because I had to hide my mounting excitement behind a very matter-of-fact exterior. I felt like I was going to burst!

Carole and I had to turn our heads away to hide our grins when Kelsey came downstairs ready for dance practice Saturday morning wearing her fluffy slippers. They were going to be quite the sensation on the plane! We gobbled down a quick breakfast and jumped in the van (we had loaded the luggage the night before while the girls were asleep).

When we arrived at the airport, I ran into the terminal, allegedly to find out about my lost bag. After a couple of minutes I came back out and told the girls that it would take about ten or fifteen minutes to retrieve the suitcase, and that the airport traffic officer had instructed me to move the van into short term parking.

"Why don't you all go in and pick out something to eat for after dance at the snack bar?" I suggested.

Carole chimed right in with, "Come on, girls. Let's go. We can use the restroom while we wait, too."

In their typical Saturday morning daze, off they strolled into the terminal, fluffy slippers and all.

I whipped the van into the parking lot and scampered back with our luggage to check in. The girls walked by after using the restroom, but didn't see me in line. I saw Carole trying her best to keep from cracking up. I hadn't expected this part of the charade to be so much fun!

Armed with boarding passes, I rushed over and met the girls at the snack bar.

"The bag is at Gate A2. We need to go up there," I reported matter-of-factly. Like good soldiers, they dutifully followed me up to the gate just as the flight was beginning to board. It wasn't until I handed our boarding cards to the gate agent and started walking down the jetway that it finally occurred to Kelsey that something odd was going on.

"Are we getting on this plane?" she asked with a look of bewilderment on her face.

Carole and I popped! Through my laughter I teased my daughters, "I wondered how much longer we could keep this going before you finally figured it out. Nice slippers, Kelsey!"

At our seats, the girls determinedly tried to get us to tell them where we were taking them. "Are we going to Charlotte to go shopping? Are we going to Disneyworld? Please tell us?" But we were having too much fun. Yes, this plane was taking us to Charlotte, but we wouldn't let on if that was our final destination.

The mystery remained unsolved for the girls when we arrived in Charlotte and made our way to the connecting gate. They saw that our next flight was to Newark, but didn't have a clue where that was. Carole and I just couldn't stop smiling.

When we were about an hour away from Newark, I casually leaned over and told Carole about the reservations I had made for the dinner show featuring "The Way Off Broadway Players." I said I had found out about it on the Internet and it looked really fun. She was enthusiastic about the idea and clearly didn't suspect any surprise.

Finally, we descended for our landing in Newark. Kelsey triumphantly declared, "I *thought* Newark was around New York City," as the skyline of Manhattan loomed before us. "We're going to go shopping in New York!" This is just about as good as it gets for a fourteen-year-old fashion magnet.

After dealing with our bags and hailing a taxi, we headed for the heart of the city. Everyone was excited as we rolled by the Statue of Liberty, the Empire State Building just in front of us. Carole and the girls still had no idea where we were staying until the cab pulled to a stop in front of the Palace Hotel. Every inch of the grand lobby oozed with elegance. I delighted in seeing Carole and the girls feeling like royalty as we made our way up to our room on the twenty-sixth floor. The view looked straight down on venerable St. Patrick's Cathedral, the most famous Catholic Church in America, with dozens of New York's classic skyscrapers sweeping all around us. This was definitely cool!

We had only enough time to clean up a bit before heading out to the Bukaru Grill. Once again I knew there was spiritual energy alive in this surprise, for I had made the reservation at The Palace six months before finding the Bukaru and had no idea where the two were located in relation to one another. When I asked the concierge for directions I was delighted to find we were only two blocks away from the restaurant. No cab necessary, we left the hotel at 4:25 and strolled leisurely over to the Bukaru by 4:30. In fact, I had to stall a bit by stopping along the way to tie my shoes so we wouldn't arrive early.

When we reached the restaurant I held the door open for Carole and the girls, not so much out of chivalry, but because I wanted to be positioned behind them so my pounding heart and bubbling excitement wouldn't give anything away. As soon as the girls stepped inside they were met by a man and woman dressed elegantly and wearing brightly colored ceramic masks. They bowed formally, handed us all playbills describing The Way-Off Broadway Players Show, and escorted us upstairs past the main dining area. Kelsey and Jenna looked a little apprehensive as they climbed the stairs because these escorts did not speak, but rather gestured and guided us through mime. Carole, on the other hand seemed quite swept up in the spirit of the action, ready to play and interact with the actors as the playbill instructed. I just tried to tag along behind with a reassuring smile for the girls and quiet anticipation for Carole. It was extra fun for me because though I knew the surprise would soon occur, I had no idea of how specifically it would be unveiled.

After what seemed like an eternity to me though it was only a few seconds, we entered the banquet room. It was a sight to behold. A beautifully decorated grand dining table stretched before us while all around danced and spun the most bizarre looking group of "performers" we'd ever seen assembled in one place at one time. Each wore a flamboyant costume with an even wilder mask. None of the actors spoke to us, though they hummed and whistled to tunes definitely of their own creation. They immediately pulled us into their midst and attempted to get us to join them in their contortions. Carole looked as though she thought this was a little odd, but fun, and went along with them. The girls, however, tightened up with unmistakable discomfort and fired one of those looks at me that said, "Dad, what have you gotten us into this time?" Carole read their body language and tried to encourage them with a smile. The whole effect was truly surreal.

After a few moments of this strange activity, the players gestured to us to sit down at the head of table. We did as instructed and then watched in mild surprise as the actors also sat down around the table. Carole spoke up playfully, "Look, isn't this neat. The performers are going to eat with us." Judging by the looks on Kelsey and Jenna's faces, this announcement was not a source of great reassurance. I'm certain at this point they would have hit the exit at a dead run if it had been up to them.

Once everyone was seated, Carole was handed a little note that read,

For the Lady . . .
The Way-Off Broadway Players welcome you to the show . . .
Kindly ask one of the Players to remove their mask. When you are ready to continue on, proceed to the next player of your choice . . .

I held my breath, desperately trying to be invisible, and watched as Carole turned to one of the actors wearing a costume reminiscent of a medieval queen and invited her to unveil herself. Ever so slowly, to build up the wonder, the actor lifted her mask. Carole let out a shriek of utter surprise and delight. "Oh my God!!! MARGIE!!!!"

I glanced quickly at Kelsey and Jenna, whose trepidation had instantly been replaced with sheer amazement. Carole seemed to be laughing and crying all at once. Immediately she asked the man standing right beside Margie to remove his mask because she could now recognize from his tall and slender build that he had to be Margie's husband Tad. Carole rushed over to these dear friends from our years in Montana and embraced them in absolute joy. I could feel every face hidden behind all those crazy masks beaming and bursting with emotion. The best part was that when Carole saw Margie and Tad, she immediately assumed that those two had driven up from Wisconsin for her birthday, but that all the others in the room were actors. She still had no idea that the entire cast of The Way Off Broadway Players were not players at all!

As Carole stood arm in arm with Margie and Tad, she was reminded to choose other players to reveal themselves. Looking across the table she pointed to the man and woman wearing the ceramic tragedy masks who had escorted us up to the banquet room. Carole's voice shot up another octave in astonishment as Muff and her husband, Zig, emerged from behind the ceramics.

I choked up with emotion when I saw Muff's reaction. She is one of the most wonderful people I have ever met. Caring, compassionate, fun, and spirited, Muff has been a true spiritual sister to Carole. Their connection runs deep, having lived together, found their husbands at just about the same time, and given birth to their daughters exactly two days apart. But through all the remarkable, magical times we had spent with Muff, I had never seen her out of control, swept away with feeling--never, until this moment. Her mouth opened, her eyes welled up with tears, and she burst. Control was out the window. Carole bounded over to her and they held one another with ardent affection. After a moment, Zig, a mountain of a man, reached around both, encircling them in a bear hug of mammoth proportion. I stole another glance at my daughters who seemed utterly mesmerized by what was unfolding before them.

One by one, Carole had the players reveal themselves. It was not until her sister, June, pulled off her Jesse Ventura mask (I didn't even know who she was under that hilarious disguise!), when it finally hit Carole that *all* of the players were actually her friends. She had been so convinced that this really was an off-Broadway show, and so completely unsuspecting that anything like this could possibly happen, that as each mask came off, her surprise heightened. She was in pure heaven, surrounded by the friends and family she loved for an evening of unbridled celebration.

These special people did so much more than show up. They all wrote letters to Carole expressing their love and describing how she had touched their lives. They brought with them a mirror they had made, encircled by a golden wreath and each gave her a little memento to hang from it that symbolized the unique and precious relationships they shared with Carole. One by one they came to the head of the table, embraced Carole, read their "love" letters and explained the meaning of their gifts.

There I stood, holding the mirror so all could see as each dear friend came forward to celebrate their love and hang their gifts on the golden wreath. In my line of sight was the woman I love more than life itself, glowing as she understood, perhaps for the first time, the difference she has made for the people she loves by simply being herself. And just beyond Carole I saw our two daughters, looking at their mother being honored as few people ever are in their lifetime. I was shaking with emotion, completely awed by the moment. Along with the births of our children and our wedding day, this was the best day of my life.

When we returned to the hotel late that night Carole pulled me aside and gently took my hand. Her eyes sparkling she spoke with great conviction.

"My life will never be the same. If I ever begin to lose faith in myself or think that I don't really matter, I'll remember this night. I love you."

This is the power of surprise with those you love. It just doesn't get any better than that.

Is it time to breakthrough in your relationships, work, and life? *Create* surprise for the people who matter to you. Surprise can be as simple as an unexpected handwritten card, or as elaborate as Carole's birthday. The key is to be sure that it is *their* surprise, not yours. To tell the truth, my idea of a terrific birthday surprise for Carole would have been to zip us off to the beach in Jamaica! But Carole loves and values friendship and family most in her life. By orchestrating a surprise that matched her highest values, the impact and joy was multiplied exponentially. To bask in the reflection of her light, and her love for friends and family, was the perfect gift for me and a WOO we will always remember.

Another secret for seizing more WOOS:
If It's Not Working, Try Something Different

Have you heard the definition of insanity? It's doing the same thing over, and over, and over again—and expecting a different result. As ridiculous as that pattern of behavior sounds, how often does that silly definition perfectly describe our almost robotic actions and conditioned responses? What habits do we insanely continue though the results of those habits are not only ineffective, but even painful, damaging, and self-defeating?

The closer you look at this principle—*If it's not working, try something DIFFERENT*—the more clear it becomes that truly living its lesson provides a powerful WOO to ignite momentum where there once was stagnation, to transform adversity into the possibility of exciting benefit.

You need look no further than the light that's illuminating the room you're in right now as you read this book (unless you're outside on a sunny day) for shining proof of the power of this simple principle. The genius who developed the electric light, Thomas Edison was the king of "if it's not working, try something different." Edison was the Michael Jordan, Tiger Woods, and Wayne Gretzky of innovation all rolled into one, with over one thousand inventions and patents, more than any individual in history has amassed. You'd think someone who produced such astonishing results must have had a tremendous academic background, yet Thomas Edison had only three months of formal education. In fact, by his late teens, Edison had lost all of his hearing in one ear, with eighty percent loss in the other. What Edison lacked in formal education and auditory capacity he more than made up for in tenacity, flexibility, and an unstoppable commitment to continually learn and grow. When speaking about the work going on in his laboratory in Menlo Park, New Jersey, he growled, "Hell, there are no rules here—we're trying to *accomplish* something."

When it came to his deafness, he turned that supposed handicap into an important ingredient in his success. He used the silence associated with deafness to sharply enhance his powers of concentration and alertness. Edison spent more than four years and experienced over four thousand failed attempts to create a functioning incandescent light bulb. But after each unsuccessful attempt, he adjusted and tried something different. After more than three years, and over three thousand failures, one of his top assistants finally reached the breaking point. Pulling his hair out and feeling angry, frustrated, and defeated, he went to Edison and asked the great inventor, "How can you *stand* all this failure?"

Edison's reply offers a sure-fire recipe for a life of wonder, light, and resilience: "Are you kidding? We just learned another way *not* to make a light bulb."

The most important place to apply this principle is in facing and dealing with fear. Ultimately, all emotions in life fall into one of two foundational categories: love or fear. The instant you choose the loving side, you feel it in every cell of your body. It is unmistakable. Mind, body, and spirit are in harmony. Life, joy, energy, and peace fill you and you know with certainty that the choice you've made is right. The physiological, emotional, and spiritual response when you choose fear is every bit as striking. There is immediate and inescapable dissonance as if the wrong key is struck on the piano.

Following the principle of "If it's not working, try something different" is of great value in virtually every facet of life. It is most powerful when it becomes a habitual way to break patterns of anger, defensiveness, and non-communication that can seriously damage our most important relationships and remove our joy.

Step Out of the Heat of the Moment

It is amazing how often we try to tackle important issues in our families at the worst possible times. When we're angry, frustrated, exhausted, or hurt, the negative energy we're feeling cannot help but spill out in the form of defensiveness, sarcasm, or confrontation. As the brilliant Eckhart Tolle explains in *The New Earth*, these negative emotions are all ego-generated and unconscious expressions of resistance. And what we resist persists.

At times of resistance, we lose sight of everything except our burning desire to prove we are right and to be validated. Again, this is the ego in full force. We tear into one another like two great rams butting heads. The result that keeps occurring in this scenario is clear. Nothing changes! Though deep down inside we want to resolve our issues, to get back on track, and to feel good again about our relationship, there is no listening, no compassion, and no progress. As Mike & the Mechanics expressed so perfectly in their classic song, "The Living Years," we all speak a different language when speaking in defense.

There is only one way this pattern will change. If it's not working, try something different. Step out of the heat of the moment and create a whole new level of connection. Set up "just listen" sessions where both of you agree to simply listen to one another for ten uninterrupted minutes. During your ten minutes, your partner can only listen—no defensiveness, no explanation, and no interjection whatsoever. And you have the same commitment to your partner. You'll be amazed at the breakthroughs and understanding that flows out of these "just listen" sessions. One of the greatest human emotional needs is to feel heard, to know that you are important and appreciated in your relationships. The "just listen" session accomplishes exactly that. You begin to truly understand how your friend, partner, child, or teammate feels. You become fully conscious, alert, and aware. This in turn sends an unmistakable energetic message and they *know* you are truly listening, truly present. Quite often that's more than enough to refresh your relationship.

A "Daley" Lesson to Live By

The last decade of my dear friend Nick Daley's life is a shining testimony to the enormous benefits we bring to ourselves and all we love when we break the patterns and habits that aren't working in our lives and try something different.

Nick had a difficult and painful childhood. His father died at a young age and when his mother remarried, Nick felt angry and cheated. He had difficulty getting along with his step-father, and when the family decided to move from Wichita Falls, Texas to Southern California, Nick, who was about to begin his junior year in high school refused to go. So, at sixteen, he lived alone in a tiny basement room he rented from a pastor who felt compassion for the lonely boy. Nick went to school each morning, to orchestra practice right after school, and then to work until ten or eleven each night. He was able to make enough money to pay his rent and to eat, but he had nothing left over.

On weekends he hustled any job he could find, from cutting grass to washing dishes, and he spent his Sunday afternoons cleaning his little apartment and getting everything ready for the week to come. His shoes had holes in them, but they were polished. His clothes were old and worn, but they were clean and pressed. He was determined, organized, and hard-working, but he was also bitter, unloved, and alone.

Through sheer resolve, Nick achieved outstanding grades in school and earned a scholarship to the University of Texas. He was driven to succeed and to show the world he could make it, that he was worthy of respect. When he married and had two lovely daughters, his sense of obligation became even stronger. But a marriage based more upon obligation than love is like a home with no furniture. It may look fine from the outside, but inside it is barren and empty. There is no comfort. The marriage failed and Nick became a single parent. Materially, he provided well for his daughters and loved them very much. But he wouldn't let his love show. There was little joy in him. He was tough, slow to give praise, and nearly incapable of expressing his affection to the very people he loved the most. For Nick, the world was like boot camp. You worked hard, you fulfilled your responsibilities, and you survived. You never abandoned others, but you never allowed yourself to get too close, either.

Although Nick achieved some financial success, he veered farther and farther from any semblance of balance. Workaholism became his norm. He began to gain weight from countless fast-food meals on the run. Though he provided a stable home for his daughters, he traveled a great deal, and even when he was home he was away. His mind was immersed in the next business meeting or challenge. Occasionally, Nick wished that he had more love, fun, and fulfillment in life. But he figured you play the hand you're dealt. In his core he knew his life wasn't working, but most of the time he kept moving so fast it was hard to notice.

When his girls were grown and ready to dive fully into their own lives he was alone again. He was on a figurative treadmill, working hard with little enjoyment, and going nowhere. The breakthrough came when it finally hit him that for things to change, *he* must change. Nick Daley decided to try something different.

For the first time, Nick began to understand that as Wayne Dyer often says, "There is no way to happiness; happiness *is* the way." Throughout his life, Nick had focused constantly on what he felt he had to do. Now he began to ask himself what he *wanted* in his life. He realized he had choices and started to make new ones. Rather than looking at the rest of his life as a battle, a war to survive, Nick decided it was time to go "4-F" and free himself from the battlefield. He chose to fill his life with *fun, fitness, family,* and *forgiveness.*

He discovered that for his life to be truly rich, it was vital for him to make his livelihood choices based upon the fun and fulfillment he would receive from his work rather than focusing so completely upon the money he would make. He bought a personal and team development seminar franchise and immersed himself in the human spirit. He excitedly dove into working with a personal coach, and was so open and enthusiastic about growing as a person he won a special award from his company for being the "Most Coachable Consultant." No one was more deserving of that honor. I know. I was his coach. For Nick, work became an opportunity to help people learn, as he had, that they really did have choices about the direction, energy, and focus of their lives. With this new motivation and inspiration, his natural wit and infectious sense of humor began to shine like a ray of pure white light. Nick Daley became glimmering proof that *fun* is available everywhere in everyone.

He also understood that without fitness, he would be too physically tired to enjoy the fun he was creating in his new life. Nick joined a Masters Swimming Program at the Aerobic Center in Dallas and transformed his body just as he had transformed his spirit. And, of course, with greater fitness came greater fun. A whole new set of friends, his swimming buddies, joined his life. He loved being the "old man" on the team and found a whole new joy in birthdays because each one moved him closer to a new older age group where he would instantly become one of the faster competitors. He became trim, strong, and vibrant.

None of the 4Fs was more important to Nick than family. His daughters were the most important people in his life, yet, as so many others do, he had somewhere fallen out of the habit of expressing his love for them. He would tease them, needle them, occasionally try to coach them, but never let all of that go and simply *love* them. He had retreated behind the assumption that they knew how he really felt about them. But in truth, they didn't know. With neglect, doubt grows.

The effect this failure to express his love to his daughters had on his own spirit had been even more destructive. Remember, the love we fail to share is the only pain we live with. Deep down in his heart, he had wanted to sweep them up in his arms as he had when they were little girls, to let that pure, free, joyous affection flow. He had ached to receive the same kind of love back from them. With the final F—forgiveness—Nick was finally able to let go of the ache and revel in the kind of loving family he had always wanted. He forgave himself for the past. The amazing power of his forgiveness was instantaneous. It was as if every cell in his body took a rich, full cleansing breath, and healed completely. His habit of withholding was replaced with loving expression.

When Nick passed away, his daughters knew without any doubt how much he loved them. They were his dearest and closest friends. He became a champion WOO-seizer because he learned that indeed, when it's not working, we can *always* try something different. Remember, seizing your WOOs and igniting your joyful spirit requires change.

Lighten Up When Others Tighten Up: Laughter Opens the WOO

If you are ready to seize more of those precious WOOs in your life, one of the most important principles to remember is to *lighten* up when you or others begin to *tighten* up. Whenever we are highly motivated to give our best, a certain degree of nervousness and heightened anticipation is both normal and usually beneficial because it helps us energize and focus. But there are times you must become aware when the butterflies in the stomach turn into buzzards, and tingling excitement into a debilitating paralysis. It's at these crucial moments that laughter is most transformational, with the power to turn trauma into triumph.

During my years as a United States Swimming Coach, I saw mirth work its magic at many pivotal moments. One was particularly memorable because it occurred at perhaps the most important competition in which two swimmers who were especially dear to me had ever participated. These two, Annie and Kim, had dreamed about their high school championship meet for years. Both had swum with me since they were young girls. High school swimming was huge to them because for the first time their non-swimmer friends would have the chance to see them shine. What's more, they were representing their school, just like the football and basketball players. (Remember, there is nothing more inspiring than having a purpose that is bigger than oneself.) To top it all off, Annie and Kim were outstanding swimmers, and break-through performances by them at these Southern California High School Championships just might impress the many college recruiters who attended this high profile meet. This was one of those WOOs in life you plan and prepare for, rather than one which spontaneously and unexpectedly occurs.

The girls were in terrific shape and perfectly rested for the finals after having qualified a week before at the preliminaries. They were ready to fly!

About twenty minutes before the start of the meet I walked over to the girls to help them focus and prepare. The moment I saw their faces I knew that the line had been passed between healthy nervous energy and total panic. They were tight as drums, and scared to the point that their confidence was beginning to drain from their spirits. After trying to inspire them with a pep talk, I could see much more drastic action was necessary. If they didn't relax and lighten up, the dream they had trained so hard for would end up a disaster.

Quickly I pulled both of them off to the side. In my best Vince Lombardi coaching voice I barked out orders to them.

"Grab your towels and wad them up tight. Good! Now, cram that wadded towel right up against your face and mouth. Do it quick! Now, I want you to scream your lungs out into that towel for thirty seconds. GO!"

They were so stunned at the suddenness of my commands they did exactly as they were told. After about 10 seconds, the silliness of it all broke through their anxiety and they started to laugh. As swimmers from other schools walked by and stared at these two goofy kids with towels in their mouths they couldn't help but laugh harder. They kept screaming into the towels just for the fun of it. They were so hilarious; I couldn't help but break up, too. Other coaches must have thought this was the strangest pre-race ritual they had ever seen.

As the girls began to settle down, the terror that had been in their eyes before our "towel therapy" transformed into lightness. Their spirits were shining once again. They had moved from fear to faith through the simple power of humor.

I will never forget that incredible day. Kim, a sophomore at the time, had always been one of those kids who did well but couldn't seem to break through to her real potential. But that afternoon she absolutely shattered her personal best times in both of her events. She placed in the top three in both and realized her lifelong dream by qualifying for the Junior Nationals. Today, more than twenty-five years later, I still cherish the vision I hold of her amazed smile when she saw what she had accomplished.

Annie had been like a daughter to me through the years that I coached her. Her father had passed away when she was twelve and I had provided her with a steady, loving, positive paternal influence through those difficult times. I'd watched her mature into a fine person and an outstanding swimmer. This was her senior year in high school, and we had focused intently on this meet, determined she would achieve her goals. In the preliminaries, she had qualified second in both the 100-yard butterfly and 100-yard backstroke. In the butterfly final, she would be swimming next to one of America's all-time greatest swimmers, Dara Torres, who had qualified first, about three full seconds ahead of Annie. I hoped with all my heart that Annie wouldn't psych herself out by worrying about being blown out of the pool by such a formidable champion.

Just before she stepped up to the starting block for the race she looked over at me one last time. I was ready. I held a crammed-up towel up to my mouth for a moment and then pulled it away to reveal an enormous grin. When I saw her light up and smile I knew her confidence had been fully restored.

In ten years of coaching her I had never seen Annie perform like she did in that 100-yard butterfly. We had hoped she would break fifty-eight seconds and believed going in that if she did everything perfectly she could pull it off. I cheered my lungs out for this wonderful girl, watching in near disbelief as she stayed right with Dara, stroke for stroke from start to finish. The two of them were a quarter of a pool ahead of the other competitors. Though Dara touched her out by a couple of tenths of a second, Annie finished with a time of 55.6 seconds—beyond our wildest dreams! She leaped out of the pool and ran to me in exultation. This time her screams were unmuffled—and of absolute joy.

Annie went on to win the 100-yard backstroke, again with a lifetime best, and received a full college scholarship to the University of California at Berkeley as a result of her tremendous performance.

As I look back on that special day, I see clearly how magical laughter at pivotal moments truly is. Seizing the WOO in any arena, from athletics to business to parenting, is about freeing the spirit. I didn't really coach swimming. I coached *people.* My purpose was to help those who I coached cross the line from fear to freedom, from failure to faith. At times, laughter is the perfect potion that makes that giant leap a shining reality.

There is another magical quality about laughter: it will help you go first!

I love my family more than life itself. They are the center of my world, the starting point for my calendar, and the source of my greatest joy. So when a speaking engagement meant that I would be two thousand miles away from my daughter Kelsey on her sixth birthday, my insides ached with guilt, disappointment, and remorse. I would be home in time for her party on the weekend, which was all that really mattered to Kelsey, but to me I couldn't help but feel that I had really let her down.

The instant that my seminar finished, I rushed to the telephone to talk with my little girl and to wish her a happy birthday. I broke into an unstoppable grin when I heard her precious voice answer the phone. Little did I know I was about to receive a lesson from this six-year old sage that I would never forget.

"Hi Kelsey! Happy Birthday, honey!" I exclaimed.

"Thank you, Daddy!"

"I miss you so much, sweetie. Tell me, what was the *best* thing that happened on your birthday?"

"Well, Mommy took me and Jenna to the *Red Robin* for dinner."

Knowing that this was one of her favorite restaurants, I figured that was her complete answer. "That's great, Kelsey. So going to the *Red Robin* was the best thing that happened all day."

Then she corrected me: "No, Daddy. That wasn't the best thing." I began to see there was more to the story.

"Well what was?" I asked, now quite curious.

"When we got to the *Red Robin* I had to go potty really bad."

I chuckled and asked her, "Now don't tell me *that* was the best thing?"

"No, Daddy!" she exclaimed in that "don't be so goofy" tone I loved so much when I teased with her.

"So what was it then?"

"Well, when I went into the bathroom, there was a *big* line of ladies waiting to use the potty."

I couldn't resist joking, "Kelsey, I certainly hope *that* wasn't the best thing that happened on your birthday."

"Oh Daddy, you're so silly. No, the best thing was when I saw the line, I told them it was my birthday, and they let me go *first!*"

Her triumph and joy was so real, I did my best to keep from cracking up until after we said goodnight and hung up the phone. Then I sat there in my hotel room rolling in laughter, completely in love with my little girl.

But as I flew home the next morning I began to see the magnificent wisdom that Kelsey had shared with me through her simple delight at moving to the head of the line. She awakened me to the truth that I, and nearly every adult I knew, would have completely missed the magic of such a birthday moment. First of all, we never would have had the confidence and exuberance to share with a line of "focused" individuals, all intent on the same "mission," that it was our birthday. Even more important, I realized we would very likely have missed the enjoyment and preciousness of a moment that for six-year-old Kelsey was better than any present. Her secret was that *she* was present for the moment, and therefore open to receive the simple joys that make life truly rich.

From that day forward, I have made it my habit to end every correspondence, e-mail, and phone message with a simple reminder of my daughter's wisdom: Remember to enjoy every precious moment. It's a thought that will move you to the front of the line in your life, where the view is the best and the possibilities the brightest. May it serve you well and help you to lighten up in all those times you tend to tighten up and find the WOO even in the most challenging of times.

Chapter 8: The Spiritual WOO

Look around you. Everywhere you look, God is there. Look within you. God is there, too. And look at the moments that take your breath away. Is there any doubt that God is there, too? In every WOO, it is God that opens the window. But it is *you* who must find the courage, energy, desire, and heart to step through that open window and live the life God has made possible for you.

To seize the Spiritual WOO, here are four wonderful practices you can adopt. These are not religious practices confined to some specific faith. They are instead spiritual practices that will elevate the quality of your life whether you're Buddhist or Baptist, Muslim or Jew, Catholic or Hindu. Gandhi said, "God is truth, no matter what you call God." When you feel connected to God you fill with a sense of optimism and possibility. As Winston Churchill said, "A pessimist sees the difficulty in every opportunity; an optimist sees the OPPORTUNITY in every difficulty." These simple practices will fill you with optimism, joy, peace, and possibility.

Spiritual WOO Practice 1:
Take time each day to be present with yourself.
Earlier in this book, I shared the vital importance of being fully present with those you love. Full presence with others lets them know they

are important. It is the single-most important ingredient in building trust in relationships. And ultimately, presence is the secret to creating balance in your life, because five minutes of full presence with a loved one is more connecting than five years of faking it. When you are more consistently present in your life you make much more of every precious moment.

It is every bit as important to take time each day to be fully present with yourself. In times of full presence with self, we connect directly with God and Spirit. For years I have practiced presence with myself in three simple yet powerful ways. First, I focus on my breathing at least ten times each day. As I take three or four rich, deep, belly breaths, the chatter in my mind ceases and I become still, conscious, and quiet.

This peaceful, focused breathing practice is perhaps the simplest form of meditation, yet I find it remarkably effective. Being fully present requires us to step out of the past and future. Our inner self-talk is always in one of those two false dimensions. You see, there is *only* the present. When we actually experienced the past, it was in that previous present moment, and when we actually arrive at the future, it will be in that later present moment. So by taking those three or four focused breaths, I create automatic present, conscious moments throughout the day. As these breathing breaks string together, I create the *habit* of presence.

The second way I practice presence is by spending about ten magical minutes each day, visualizing my abundance affirmations. For me, it is a time of complete immersion and surrender. I always emerge feeling refreshed, peaceful, and balanced.

Lastly, I have used running and exercise as a presence practice for more than twenty years. When I run, I am completely quiet. I purposely de-focus, allowing my thoughts to flow freely with no outcome or objective in mind. I call this my "percolator" time. By letting go of any effort to force concentration or accomplish anything specific, I am completely free, present, and conscious. It never ceases to amaze me that when I return from a run or a workout how clear I become without trying to find clarity.

Your regular practice of presence with yourself can take many forms. Prayer, meditation, gardening, listening to your iPod, yoga, swimming, walking, or affirmation and visualization are all wonderful possibilities for you to explore to find your ideal practice. It is far less important how *long* you spend on your practice as it is how *often* you practice—ideally, it will be *consistent,* for at least a few minutes daily.

As you develop the habit of daily present time with yourself, you will find one of its most important benefits. A metaphor from my years as a swimming coach reveals this potent value. In swimming, there are two phases to each arm stroke. The part of the stroke that is underwater, where the swimmer is actually pulling the water through, underneath the body, is called the "resistance" phase, because the athlete is using muscle and energy to drive the weight and pressure of the water backward in order to propel forward. The goal of the resistance phase is to move as much water as powerfully and efficiently as you possibly can. I liken the resistance phase of swimming to the go-go-go, get-things-done aspects of life. These parts of life require focus, energy, strength, and determination as we deal head-on with pressures and challenges.

There is a second phase to each arm stroke, however, which is the yin to the yang of resistance. This is the part of the stroke that begins when the swimmer lets go of the resistance and lifts the arm above the water, rotating it back out in front of the body, sliding the arm forward until the next "catch" when resistance begins again. This is called the "recovery" phase of the arm stroke. The goal of this phase is effortlessness. It is to completely let go of resistance and to allow the arm and body a chance to replenish and revive. The recovery phase of your life is the time you take to be present with yourself.

Most coaches and athletes focus the vast majority of their attention on the resistance phases. At first glance, these active, goal-oriented phases seem to be more important because effectiveness at resistance is immediately visible and clear. You can see and measure the results and accomplishments. But the truth is, if you are not equally effective in your recovery phase, eventually you will burn out.

Similarly, you may have the flashiest cell phone on the market, with every bell and whistle you could dream of. But if you don't purchase the appropriate re-charger and plug that phone and charger into a dependable source of power, that phone is going to have a very short life. Whenever you let go and are present with yourself, you immediately plug your spiritual re-charger into the most powerful source of energy, vibration, peace, and joy. That source is God, Spirit, Creator . . . there are many names but only one essence. And just as five minutes of full presence with loved ones sends them the unmistakable message that they are loved and important, a few moments of daily connection with God through presence with yourself opens your heart and awareness to the same truth about yourself. You are *loved.* Who you *are* makes a difference.

Spiritual WOO Practice 2: See God in DIFFERENCES!

When he was asked to define his religion, the Dalai Lama simply replied, "Compassion." The essence of what makes this remarkable man such an example of true spirituality is his ability to see God in differences. In fact, as he looks at those who have oppressed him and his people, when he sees anger and even inhumanity, he immediately sees the connection we all share rather than the separation. Just as he sees God's love in those he is closest to, he sees that same presence in every one of God's children, even those with views completely different than his own.

Many people have a strong desire to be around only those who are "like-minded." We fear and avoid differences as if they are the most heinous evils imaginable. But to expand spiritually and truly grow as a human being, one of the most powerful steps you can take is to challenge yourself to become more open, respectful, and interested in differences.

When you look at any great athletic team, any high performing business, or any magnificent cast of actors in an award winning film, it is the differences and contrasts that create the synergy and depth that makes the whole richer and more powerful. As a vice-president of a large air freight company and again as the vice-president of a major training company, I wanted to surround myself with plenty of teammates who saw the things that I missed, whose strengths filled in for my weaknesses. If I had chosen to only have "like-minded" colleagues around me, we would have seen only what I saw. With the different styles, talents, and vision, we were able to see and do so much more. The key was to truly *respect* those differences and to understand that we could, as Coach John Wooden so perfectly put it, "disagree without being disagreeable." In fact, I came to truly marvel at those differences that were so beyond my style and focus. I recognized that there were often times when those differences in approach were absolutely necessary if we were to succeed.

In many of the churches I have visited over the years, even those that I love and have attended regularly, I have found it disappointing that there is a sense of exclusion and separation. Though it is sometimes subtle, there is ongoing verbal and nonverbal communication which says in effect, it's us against them. In other words, we're different from everyone else and those others are therefore to be disdained, kept at arm's length (or longer), or are flat out wrong. And yet the greatest of all teachers, Jesus, through his words and actions exemplified compassion and understanding for those who were different.

In fact, if you look closely at the foundational principles of virtually all of the world's religions, there are so many similarities. In these areas of similarity, we find the true heart of these religions. When we see these connections and similarities, it becomes much more likely we will generate understanding, respect, admiration, and at the very least, genuine tolerance rather than fear, suspicion, and distrust. Even when we look for God in differences, every individual and family will still choose their primary faith center and build great relationships with their spiritual community. However, with this new understanding, we evolve spiritually, just as Mother Teresa advocated when she said: "There is only one God and He is God to all; therefore it is important that everyone is seen as equal before God. I've always said we should help a Hindu become a better Hindu, a Muslim become a better Muslim, a Catholic a better Catholic. To God, everything is simple—God's love for us is greater than all the conflicts, which will pass."

Seeing God in differences is a clear indicator that you believe in abundance rather than scarcity. With this belief, it becomes natural for your spirit to be open and free rather than guarded and restrictive. In this way, an abundance mentality ignites possibility-thinking, optimism, faith, and joy. When you look for God in differences it doesn't mean you will no longer be drawn to those who are like you and with whom you easily and naturally click. It will not diminish the special closeness you feel in your most loving relationships. It will simply mean that when you see differences you will create the habit of replacing fear and distrust with curiosity, interest, and above all, compassion. You will recognize that when you seek to understand differences you will give yourself the WOO to expand your thinking, heighten your awareness, and truly grow.

My wife, Carole, is so different from me in many ways. She is at ease and comfortable at parties and social events even when we hardly know anyone present. I am awkward and anxious from the moment we receive the invitation to attend such events. Our energies are exactly reversed when it comes to public speaking, where I am in my element and she must summon great courage. Carole has been fascinated with natural health and nutrition for thirty years. Before I met her, my idea of healthy eating was being sure I ate my pickle with my double cheeseburger and fries to satisfy my vegetable requirement for the day! I have an unstoppable belief in abundance while Carole grew up in a very frugal family that worried about money and watched every penny. Another area of major difference with us concerns time. Carole is extremely easy-going about time. She has no problem being twenty or thirty minutes late. I break out in a cold sweat if I haven't arrived at an appointment at least fifteen minutes early.

Yet, despite all these polar opposites we have built a wonderful marriage because we have learned to see God in our differences. I have let go of my obsessive need to be early and Carole has made a real effort to be more conscious of when it's important to be on time. I have made dramatic changes in my eating habits and have even made significant improvements in my comfort level in social situations. Carole has become much more abundance-oriented, exercises far more consistently, and has made great strides in breaking through her fear of public speaking. Without one another's differences and our willingness to embrace the value and possibility in them, these expansions in our lives and overall happiness would never have occurred.

Spiritual WOO Practice 3: Giving Without the Desire to Be Repaid

One of the simplest and most fulfilling ways to seize the spiritual WOO is to give without the desire to receive in return. Mother Teresa said, "Service is love in action." When you give without the desire for repayment, you instantly access love. It is a sure-fire way to fill up with spiritual joy. Giving anonymously, giving sincere third-party compliments, or simply telling others what you admire, respect, and appreciate about them are powerful ways to give with no thought about what will be returned to you.

When you give without the desire to be repaid, you *will* be repaid in abundance. It is spiritual law. **And when the repayment comes, in whatever form, it is essential that you graciously and happily receive.** If you don't receive with sincere appreciation, you snatch the giver's joy of giving away. The key, however, is to allow the spiritual law to manifest as it will, without trying to force the law into motion. When you receive your ultimate joy from the act of giving, you hold the key to true happiness. The most beautiful expression of this Spiritual WOO practice comes from St. Francis of Assisi:

> Lord, make me an instrument of your peace.

Where there is hatred, let me sow love,
Where there is injury, pardon,
Where there is doubt, faith,
Where there is despair, hope,
Where there is darkness, light,
And where there is sadness, joy.
Oh Divine Master, please grant that I may not so much
Seek to be consoled as to console,
To be understood, as to understand,
And to be loved, as to love.
For it is in giving that we receive,
It is in pardoning that we are pardoned,
And it is in dying that we are born to eternal life.

I visualize and affirm this magnificent prayer every day of my life. It is my first focus as I rise each morning to begin the day. As each phrase reaches my heart, I feel it open. As a professional speaker, I have a simple ritual just before I begin every presentation. First, I recite St. Francis' prayer. Then I touch laminated photo pages of Carole, Kelsey, and Jenna. Instantly, I am inspired to serve and to give without any need or thought of repayment. Create your own ritual to remind yourself to give without the desire for repayment. You will become an open vessel through which God will flow to all that you touch.

Spiritual WOO Practice 4: Smile!

Right now as you're reading, please put a big smile on your face! I know that's an unusual request, but I'm not kidding. As Forrest Gump would say, "for no particular reason," just smile!

What do you notice in your spirit the instant you smile? How does a smile make you feel? Isn't it amazing how the act of smiling isn't merely an activation of tiny facial muscles that lift the edges of your mouth? It's so much more. As soon as you smile it's as if your entire being becomes lighter. In that magical moment there is no complicated past, no uncertain future, only a joyful now.

We are conditioned to smile only in response to some cause. This Spiritual WOO practice encourages you to make smiling a proactive cause rather than a reactive effect. Several years ago, I had the privilege of attending a session for a group of cancer patients led by Dr. Norman Cousins, the author of *Anatomy of an Illness.* When he was thirty years old, Dr. Cousins was diagnosed with a leukemia-like disease with no known cure and an extremely high likelihood of death. There was no treatment or procedure for this terminal disease. But Cousins refused to accept this dire diagnosis. He knew himself to be a spiritual being residing in a physical body. Therefore, he reasoned, any cure would need to be spiritually focused. He decided to attack his disease with enormous doses of joy. For weeks he spent his days watching old black-and-white slapstick movies from Charlie Chaplin to Laurel and Hardy. His friends and family must have thought he had become delirious! But somehow Cousins understood intuitively that his immune system seemed to gather power whenever he was truly happy. He could feel it in every one of his ninety trillion cells. Dr. Cousins literally smiled and laughed himself to health.

When I saw him at this event he was in his seventies. In a room that easily could have been permeated with fear and despair, his sparkling eyes and ever-present smile simply overwhelmed all negativity. I marveled that Dr. Cousins' facial lines had all formed in the upward curve of a smile. He didn't need to say a word to lift every spirit there that night. His smile was more than enough.

Have you ever had one of those days where "for no particular reason" you just feel like smiling? As you walk by people who normally would have been as invisible as air to you, you now connect, and they automatically smile back in return. It's as if you flick on a light within each person you meet through your radiant spirit. What you don't see is that your smile sets off a chain reaction as each person who has been freshly ignited through your glow touches others. Your smile has set off a wave of positive energy that is as impossible to stop as the ripple effect created when you throw a stone into a pond. When you smile, however, the ripple effect does not only move out away from you. The waves move just as irresistibly inward, into your soul and heart. The result is creativity, lightness, and an insatiable belief in possibility.

There are of course times when you will not wish to smile and even when it would be seen as inappropriate or insensitive. But it is truly a rare person who smiles too much. This Spiritual WOO practice is about creating the discipline to smile, which if practiced consistently, will lead to the habit of smiling.

It is my belief that God wants us to smile.

Seizing the WOO—It's all about BREAKING THROUGH!

As a professional speaker, I am known as "America's Breakthrough Coach!" I love this title because I believe passionately that we are all in the business of breaking through. Whether we're moving from fear to freedom, from failure to faith, from angst to awareness, or from ego to "we-go," seizing the WOO requires us to move beyond limits, obstacles, fears, or doubts. Every day as parents, we are in the breakthrough business, teaching our children to make good choices that will lead them to confidence, compassion, and happiness. In our professional careers we are seeking to move to the next level in terms of challenge, responsibility, contribution, and abundance. When it comes to our health, our breakthroughs in diet, exercise, attitude, and habits will determine the way we feel every single day. And in our relationships our breakthroughs in communication, patience, presence, understanding, openness, and trust make all the difference.

Ultimately, all breakthroughs are the same. They are those precious moments when we move from fear to love. Fear can take many forms, such as uncertainty, ego, worry, doubt, anger, defensiveness, and procrastination. Love, too, has many forms including peace of mind, gratitude, faith, consciousness, abundance mentality, understanding, and kindness. When you detach and observe that all breakthroughs occur when we move from fear to love, a remarkable truth emerges. All fears are illusions based upon the past or the future. They are either in the form of negative emotions and thoughts about something that has already happened or worried anticipation about something that has not yet occurred. All *loving* emotions are in the present. They require present consciousness and awareness. So in a very powerful sense, all breakthroughs are moving beyond the past or future into the present where there is only love.

The ancient Chinese sage Confucius once said, "When we hear we forget. When we see we remember. But when we *do* we understand." In my seminars, I don't want participants to simply hear about the concept or see an example of breaking through. I want them to actually experience it. So the seminar finishes with the remarkable "Breakthrough Experience" as every participant is given the opportunity to break through a one-inch thick wooden board karate-style!

You read about this experience earlier in the book, as I described how the power of team helped Anik crash through her board. On that day, as on every day when I lead this exercise, everyone there wrote on their one-inch thick wooden boards, inscribing something they truly wanted to move beyond in their life – a limit, fear, obstacle, habit, or doubt.

The meaning participants in this exercise give to their breakthrough metaphor creates the power in the experience. For some, it's fear of failure. For others, it's procrastination, anger, stress, rejection, or loss. On the other side of the board, participants get to be kids again. Filled with the no-limit possibility-thinking they had when they were children, the participants write down what's waiting for them when they've broken through and left that limit in the dust where it belongs. The process of board breaking empowers people to be their best when their best is called for and teaches them about balance physically, mentally, emotionally, and spiritually.

Clearly, board-breaking also creates an unforgettable experience of real teamwork. Picture again how all team members cheer for each other at the tops of their lungs. The unconditional support and energy is *astonishing*! The place is shaking, energy is soaring, and music is pounding. And when each person breaks his or her board, it is a moment of unrivaled clarity, focus, and celebration. For many people, it's the first time they've ever had a room full of people cheer for them and focus completely on their success. The powerful emotional experience of the breakthrough becomes a source of confidence, courage, and energy for the participants to draw upon as they tackle their real-life obstacles, fears, habits, and doubts from that amazing moment on.

After having been immersed in this breakthrough focus for two decades, it has become clear to me that there are two pivotal areas of potential breakthrough that have the most profound impact on our lives. Once you move beyond these two key obstacles, you will seize many more WOOs that will bring you great peace of mind, wonderful relationships, and a life of abundance, joy, and true fulfillment.

WOO Obstacle 1: The Need for Approval

For many people, the need for approval is the single greatest barrier to peace of mind and joy. It can become more addictive than a drug, because once you move from simply appreciating recognition, acknowledgement, and praise to craving these outside validations, you can never get enough.

Fear of rejection is the fuel that powers the need for approval. As outside approval becomes a deep-seated need in your ego, you become a slave to your reputation and what others think about you. The internal motivations that drive your actions are thoughts about what you'll get rather than what you can give. There is no chance to access the fulfillment that resides in the present moment because your thoughts are always looking ahead for that future praise. When you do receive that occasional morsel of recognition, it is hungrily consumed but never fully satisfying. You wonder what will happen if you're not as good tomorrow as you were today. The cycle spins out of control until you lose all sight of who you really *are*.

In the first few years of my career as a professional speaker, I lived and died for the participant evaluations. As soon as the seminar was over, I couldn't wait to read these comments and ratings. I would rush off to some quiet corner and devour every single evaluation. And what was I looking for? In a word: *perfection*. Anything less than one hundred percent validation left me crushed with a feeling of complete rejection.

As I look back now, it's really quite humorous. Because my programs are very positive, fun, and engaging, virtually everyone rated the seminar at the highest level. But there were always one or two who would give it a four out of five, or heaven forbid even a three. As soon as I found those one or two less than spectacular reviews all the others meant absolutely nothing. No passionately positive comment could stand up to that one less-than-stellar rating. In my ego, I had failed and been summarily rejected.

This wasn't just a momentary disappointment. The impact it had on me physically was intense and lasting. My chest tightened and my stomach tied up in knots. I was as exhausted as if I'd just run a marathon. For days and days I'd see the evaluation in my mind and those same intense feelings would return. Eventually my thoughts would turn to the next event and some of the intensity would wane. But instead of thinking about how I could serve and what I could give, all of those emotions would congeal into an even more extreme drive to receive adulation. And so it went in a continuous cycle.

So how do you break through this paralyzing need for approval? As with all ego-based challenges, the first step is awareness. For me, the breakthrough was one of the most transformational moments in my life. After finishing a half-day seminar in St. Louis, I rushed off to the airport and immediately pulled out the participant evaluations. Did they love me this time? Was my score perfect or had someone seen me as less than wonderful? Literally shaking with desperate anticipation like an addict needing his fix, I tore into the reviews when suddenly a strange question popped into my mind. I asked myself, *Why am I doing these seminars? What is my true motivation and purpose?*

The questions jolted me into the present moment where I could detach and see the truth. Instantly I saw clearly that my speaking had been completely focused on receiving approval. I became aware that this need for external validation was insatiable and could never be satisfied. And then I realized that what I truly loved most in my speaking wasn't to be found in the response at all. What gave me the ultimate "juice" was the heightened alertness and sense of being completely in the flow of the present moment that filled me when I was speaking and teaching. It was effortless and energizing, as if God was speaking through me. With this fresh consciousness that my real purpose was to simply be present when I spoke, it felt as if a gigantic weight had been lifted from my spirit. I was suddenly light and energized, whereas moments before I had been bone tired.

From that day forward, I never asked for evaluations again. Participants still offered feedback, comments, and appreciation as much or more than ever. But I no longer focused on this input through the ego-driven lens of a rating scale. It became natural to replace the need for approval with simple gratitude. In fact, this is the secret to breaking through the need for approval—to replace dependence with appreciation. I truly appreciated the wonderful positive comments I received, but no longer blew them out of proportion. Similarly, I no longer died from constructive criticism. Instead I felt thankful for the opportunity to learn from perspectives and ideas that differed from my own. What really mattered to me was that feeling of sublime presence that filled me when I spoke.

No matter how long you have been tormented by the need for approval, you can seize the WOO and breakthrough now by first becoming aware of that need and then by replacing dependence with gratitude. Rather than responding to praise with false humility, you'll receive recognition with heartfelt thanks and then you'll let it go. You'll no longer take criticism personally as a form of rejection. Instead, you'll be able to detach and consider the different viewpoint as a gift that can ignite fresh ideas.

When you release the need for approval you will also discover that comparison with others no longer matters to you. Comparison is a form of judgment driven by the ego's compulsion to feel superior. You will find it tremendously freeing to let go of the unquenchable thirst to be "the" best, which always leaves you at the mercy of other's evaluations, and instead focus on giving 'your" best in the present moment.

Many parents can fall into the destructive habit of using comparison as a way to motivate their children. Statements like "You should act more like your sister," or "Your brother wouldn't do that!" tear down your children's self-esteem and fuels their need for outside approval to feel worthy. If you practice comparison enough as a parent, your children will never feel they are good enough in your eyes. This fear of not measuring up will follow them wherever they go. In business, many managers and executives use the same approach of comparing employees to one another to motivate and ignite performance, with the same damaging results. The truth is there is no need to use comparison in your parenting or leading. Instead you can simply focus on helping others make better choices and behave positively. Letting go of comparison doesn't mean you can't learn from others by examining best practices and successful solutions to challenges. The key is to no longer place those you lead on some sort of rating scale. You can help them learn that giving their best and being fully conscious in the present moment is perfect, complete, and deeply satisfying. In this way you will guide them to peace of mind, confidence, and appreciation rather than envy. You will create an environment both at home and at work that moves from ego to "we go!"

WOO Obstacle 2: The Need to Control Other People

For many years, I have attended an amazing community church here in Asheville, North Carolina called Jubilee. Every Sunday, the instant I walk through the doors of this humble, funky, fun-loving little church, I feel extraordinarily light, at ease, and free. It's a completely different feeling than I've had at any other church or gathering place. For quite some time I puzzled over what it was about Jubilee that created this powerful and immediate impact on my spirit. At first I thought it was the wonderful music that lifted my soul. But then I noticed the same feelings were present even when the music had not yet started. Perhaps it was the remarkable sense of community that filled the room. Everywhere I looked people were embracing, smiling, and connecting. It was as if the Jubilants were actually one very large family. But then I realized that the feeling struck me even before I reached the meeting area. Perhaps these extraordinary feelings were generated because of the minister, Howard Hanger, and his special spirit. I consider Howard a truly great human being, one of my real-life heroes. He is brilliant, kind, gentle, open, loving, and humble with a fabulous sense of humor and endless heart. But then I remembered that I felt exactly the same feelings when Howard was away and someone else was there to fill in for him. What was it about Jubilee that had this unique effect on me?

And then one Sunday morning it finally hit me. It wasn't the music, the camaraderie, or even Howard. It was that Jubilee is an organization that has broken through the need to control other people. All Jubilants are honored and appreciated for who they are and free to be themselves. It is the most egoless environment I've ever experienced. Everyone involved with running Jubilee has released any obsession with perfection and replaced this restrictive, controlling spirit with a simple faith that all will be well.

It starts with Howard's comfortable leadership. Howard loves to deliver his Sunday messages and to orchestrate the spiritual rituals and ceremonies that are integral parts of each celebration. In addition to being a minister, Howard is a professional musician and relishes performing and interacting with audiences. But he has absolutely no interest in the financial, administrative, and logistical operations of the church. So those are handled comfortably and joyfully by someone else who is passionate about operations. Howard's only participation in those areas is to say thank you! The various teams that add immensely to the sense of community at Jubilee such as the Service Team or the

Arts Team are led by volunteers with great zeal for those programs. And so this energizing, comfortable, and free attitude permeates the community. If you have an interest or idea at Jubilee, you are encouraged to take the ball and run with it.

Building a spiritual community that is free of the need for control has created a remarkable effect. The participation level in the community at Jubilee is off the charts! Virtually every Jubilant is involved in at least one team. Every person who wants to sing, dance, play an instrument, or recite poetry during a service is welcomed and encouraged regardless of their skill and experience. Some of the most moving moments at Jubilee for me have been when someone seized the WOO and performed for the very first time in front of a crowd of people. Though their hands were shaking and a note or two may have missed the right key, their courage and desire to give something straight from their hearts always left me teary-eyed and inspired. And, at Jubilee you can bet that that first-time performer received a standing ovation.

Conversely, when you have a compulsive need to control others, the people around you are terrified to make mistakes. And, of course, what you focus on is what you create. Performance will suffer and morale will tumble. Eventually they will either leave you, your family, or your organization, or simply fade into ambivalence where the goal is no longer to contribute, innovate, or take positive risks, but rather to stay as safe and uninvolved as possible.

The need to control others is driven by the ego's desperate obsession with having to be right. To the ego, being wrong is the equivalent of death. When you become aware of this subversive need and make the conscious decision to choose to be at peace and at ease rather than to have to be right, life transforms from a struggle into a beautiful dance. You discover a rhythm with those around you and balance within yourself.

Years ago, I was vice-president/general manager of a personal development and team-building seminar company near San Diego, California. When my team and I attended an experiential learning program at a ropes course, it proved to be a WOO that opened my eyes to the futility of trying to control other people. The goal of the program that day was to bring us closer together as a team, and the most powerful lesson for me came on an apparatus called the "commitment bridge."

On this element, you and your partner climb up a telephone pole to a height of twenty-five feet. Suspended at that height are two cables that stretch from the telephone pole in a v-shape attaching to two other poles about thirty feet distant. These two poles are placed ten feet apart. The challenge for you and your partner is to support each other with your hands pressed against one another's as you gradually inch your way along the cables with the goal of reaching the twin poles at the far end. So with each step you take, the cables are farther and farther apart and you are forced to lean into each other at an ever-increasing angle. If you make it all the way to the end of the cables you and your partner will be practically laid out horizontally with your bodies suspended twenty-five feet off the ground like Superman in flight looking down on Metropolis!

My partner was a young woman who was at best five-foot-two. My first instinct as we began to teeter our way along the cables was that as the bigger and stronger of the two, I would need to take charge and control the action. But the effect of my dominance was to simply throw us more and more off balance. By the time we had moved the first five feet along the cables it became crystal clear that if I kept to this strategy we were going to crash fast. The only way we were going to make progress was to commit to one another equally and to let go of any thought of control. We had to completely trust that we each could supply just the right amount of support that the other needed to maintain balance. The farther we progressed the more we needed to trust and the more we had to let go of any thought of controlling the other. It was incredible! We were each so completely present and connected that we began to move as one. We made it over three quarters of the way across the cables before we lost it and were eased down to the ground by our harnesses. The instant we landed, our teammates swept us up in celebration.

The more I thought about the experience the more I began to see that very often in my life I had been trying to dominate and control others as I had done with my partner as we set off along the cables. For the first time I understood that the effect of this need to control was not only to stifle the potential and creativity of those around me, but to weaken myself just as it had on the commitment bridge. If I could not trust others I couldn't truly trust myself. The WOO closes fast when there is no trust to hold it open.

A couple of weeks after the ropes course I facilitated what I considered to be the most important meeting we would ever have at my company because we were to determine our team vision statement. My normal approach to the meeting would have been to control the process. I had come up with what I thought to be a good idea for the vision statement and would have led everyone one way or another to buy into my outcome. But the experience of the commitment bridge had opened my eyes to the truth that an effective and inspiring vision had to be one that was created and owned by the team, not one that was dictated by me. And so I put my trust in my team and facilitated the process rather than controlled it. I asked rather than told, encouraged rather than dominated. The result was magnificent. I had never seen my entire team so fully engaged in a meeting. It was a perfect example of moving from ego to "we go." We emerged from the process with a vision statement that everyone owned personally and that reflected simply and powerfully what we aspired to be. Nearly twenty years since the day we defined our vision, the statement is still as fresh in my mind as if it were yesterday. This simple five-word affirmation perfectly expresses the result of letting go of the need to control other people:

We are champions of empowerment.

Isn't this exactly what we want to be for our children, spouses, partners, friends, and ourselves? If you value freedom for yourself, you must give it to others. You must let go of the reins of control and fully trust. Only then can you truly empower rather than over-power. You will find that your influence grows rather than weakens.

After attending one of my seminars, a doctor named Paul powerfully expressed what letting go of the need to control others can mean to a family. Paul and his wife Julie had raised their children with great devotion. They did all they knew how to create a home filled with love, kindness, and caring discipline. They were committed to instilling strong values and personal responsibility into the hearts and minds of their children. But as the kids became teenagers and wanted more freedom and trust (as all teenagers do!), Paul found it increasingly difficult to let go of the reins of control. He found his relationship with his oldest son, John, was more often abrasive rather than embracive. Their home was often filled with the pressure and tension that always accompanies a battle for control.

Everything came to a head when John announced at twenty-one that he was going to marry his college sweetheart. Paul was convinced they were much too young for marriage and did everything in his power to stop them. But what you resist persists. When John defied his father's wishes, Paul slammed the door shut and refused to have anything to do with his son and his young wife. That door stayed locked shut for eight long years. John and his wife moved to Colorado and started their own family, bringing two beautiful children into this world. Paul neither spoke with his son nor saw his only grandchildren.

The love we fail to share is the only pain we live with. When you are driven by the need to control other people, love is withheld and pain becomes your constant companion. Though Paul continued with his life as a highly successful doctor and a devoted husband to Julie and father to his other children, he could cover up the gaping wound in his spirit but not heal it.

At the seminar, Paul finally faced the pain that his need for control had created. His wooden board represented the misplaced pride and obsession with having to be right that had eaten a hole in his heart.

On the other side of the board he envisioned a loving relationship with John and the joy he would feel as a grandparent. When he broke his board that afternoon, eight years of repressed agony was released and tears flowed unashamedly. Within minutes of the close of the seminar Paul seized the WOO and called his son. He humbled himself and asked for John's forgiveness and the chance to make a fresh start.

Today John has moved his young family back to North Carolina so his children can grow up near their loving grandparents. They see Paul and Julie nearly every day. Paul has come to adore John's wife and to deeply admire and respect the way she and John are raising the children. Paul has powerfully opened a WOO with his family that has brought him the greatest joy he has ever known. This kind of freedom and lasting joy awaits you as soon as you let go of your need to control others.

Chapter 9
Who You Are Makes a Difference

Throughout this book, we have learned secrets in each of the key areas of *energy, livelihood, the relay paradigm,* and *the window of opportunity* that can bring fresh joy to our spirits. But, ultimately, joy is a choice that can only flourish when we understand that each of us is important and that we have the chance to make a genuine difference in the lives of others. A true story about a wonderful teacher named Helice Bridges powerfully demonstrates how this thread of hope weaves its magic through our lives.

Though Helice taught high school English, she realized that she really taught *people* rather than just a subject. Her ultimate purpose was to help her students learn to think creatively, flexibly, and confidently so they would grow to trust and believe in themselves. Such a compelling purpose ignites truly enabling questions. As she focused on her vision for these young people she asked herself, *How can I help them know that who they are makes the difference?*

When you ask an enabling question, be prepared for some life-changing answers. Helice's answer came to her as a wonderful plan for a unique ceremony. She decided that each semester on the last day of school, she would bring each of her students to the front of the class and give them a little blue ribbon. On the ribbon she had printed,

Who I Am Makes a Difference. As the students stepped forward to receive their ribbons, Helice honored them by telling personal stories about each one. All semester long, Helice had looked carefully into the hearts and minds of these young people, searching for the special, unique, and powerful qualities that shone in each of them. By creating the ribbon ceremony, Helice became an inspiring and positive who-said of the greatest magnitude, often seeing the genius and greatness in these young men and women before they had seen it in themselves. The celebration became a rite of passage for them, a moment to step up to a higher level of inner faith. When she spoke about each student as she awarded the ribbons, her words touched their hearts and lifted them up so they felt about ten feet tall. She helped them become certain of what they had previously only hoped might be true.

She conducted the ceremony for a couple of years, and the students absolutely loved it. They wore their ribbons all day and felt great. For many, it changed the entire direction of their lives. The results were so encouraging she began to wonder what would happen if she took the idea a step further. So the next semester she held the celebration just as she had in the past but decided this time to add a new dimension.

At the end of the ceremony when Helice had given ribbons to all of her students, she said, "You've earned these ribbons because who you are *does* make a difference. Wear your ribbon for the rest of the day, and remember how important and remarkable you are. Then let's find out what happens when we take our ceremony and extend it beyond our classroom. I want you to look at the people in your life who have made a difference for you. Take a moment to connect with them, and give them the ribbon. As you pin it on, tell them *why* they made such a positive difference. Ask them if they would wear the ribbon for a day and then pass it on, asking the next person to whom they give the ribbon to do the same. Let's see how far it goes. Maybe one of those ribbons will go all the way around the world and end up right back with you. Let's see what happens."

The kids thought that was a pretty neat idea. One young man had received great attention and support from a junior executive at a career day. Despite his busy schedule the executive had continued to keep in touch with the student, becoming a true friend and mentor. After receiving his ribbon from Helice, the student walked into the young executive's office and gave him the award. Filled with joy and appreciation he said, "Who you are has made a big difference for me. You didn't have to do all that stuff. You really went the extra mile. You make me feel like I'm somebody! I can't thank you enough. Would you wear this ribbon and then when you've worn it for a day, would you give it to someone else who's made a difference for you?"

The young executive hugged the young man and, smiling broadly, said, "You bet! I'd be honored to wear the ribbon. Thank you!"

So all day long the young executive proudly wore his blue ribbon feeling the inner satisfaction of knowing that at least for this boy, the words on his ribbon rang true—*Who I Am Makes a Difference.* That evening he asked himself to whom he would give the ribbon. Before he went to sleep he made his decision. So the next morning, he asked if he could have a word with his boss, the founder and CEO of the company. Though widely respected as a very successful businessman, the CEO was not a very popular character. He was tough and demanding, a perfectionist who rarely smiled, with a demeanor as unyielding and cold as stainless steel.

Despite his boss's reputation, the young executive walked into his office with great anticipation and sat down across from him. He said, "I wanted to show you something I received yesterday. Look at this great ribbon. One of the students I met at the high school career day came into the office yesterday. He's a terrific young man. I've helped him with some school projects and spent some time with him just talking. Anyway, he brought this ribbon to me yesterday and said that who I am makes a difference. Then he told me that I'm supposed to give the ribbon to somebody else who's made a difference for me. Well, when I asked myself who I should give it to, I knew I wanted to give it to you, sir."

The CEO was taken aback and wondered what the young executive wanted. The young executive went on to say, "I don't know if anybody knows you well, and I'm not sure I do. But there's no question that you're a creative genius. Because of that creative genius, I'm blessed with a job I love in a field that is just right for me. So you've made a big difference for me and I just wanted to say thanks. Would you wear this ribbon?"

Suddenly, the curmudgeon actually smiled and asked, "Do you really mean it?"

The executive said, "I sure do."

The CEO responded quietly, "I'd be happy to wear this ribbon." As he pinned it on his chest, the CEO felt a new glow inside. All that day the employees in the office kept trying to figure out what was up with the boss—he was out walking around and smiling! He strolled around the office stopping to talk with people and thank them for their efforts and diligence. They thought, "Gee, what happened? Profits must be way up or something."

As he drove home that night, the CEO asked himself, "Who do I want to give the ribbon to?" As soon as he asked, the answer burst from his heart. When he arrived home, he walked straight to his fourteen-year-old son's bedroom and knocked gently on his door. The boy invited him in, and he walked over and sat down beside his son. Glancing first down at the ribbon he held in his hand, and then looking straight into his son's eyes, the CEO pointed to his ribbon and said, "Look what I received today. One of the young execs in the office came up to me this morning and gave me this ribbon. He said that I had made a big difference in his life. He called me a creative genius. Can you believe that?" As he spoke the man was filled with joy.

Then he continued, "He told me I'm supposed to keep this ribbon ceremony going—I'm supposed to give it to someone else. So as I drove home tonight, I asked myself, who makes a difference for me? Immediately I knew the person I need to give this ribbon to is *you*, son.

"You know, most of the time all I ever do is get on your back. I ask you why you don't get a haircut, why you don't do your homework, why you don't clean up your room, why you don't do this or that. But when I started to think about who's made a difference for me, I realized how much I love you and how seldom I tell you. I wanted you to know that, along with your mom, you're the most important person who's ever been in my life. Will you wear this ribbon?"

The boy started to cry. Not just a little—he sobbed out of control and couldn't stop. His dad didn't know what to do, but wrapped his arms around him and rocked him, letting him cry.

Finally, the boy cried himself out. His dad looked at him with love and concern and asked, "Son, why were you crying?"

The boy looked up at his father through red, weary eyes and said, "Dad, I've been so upset I felt like I was breaking up inside. I had decided that tomorrow I would kill myself—I didn't see any reason to live. I didn't think you loved me. Now I don't have to, Dad. I'll wear your ribbon. I love you, Dad."

I don't know if each window of opportunity is going to have that kind of impact for you and those you love, but remember that it *could*. Remember, when you look at each moment as a WOO you take a quantum leap toward building a joyful spirit. The happiness you'll discover as you make new choices to elevate your energy, to create a livelihood that's in concert with your values, to become a full-out player in the Relay Paradigm, and to live your life as a true contributor will automatically ignite new joy in everyone you touch. Who you are makes a massive difference!

Enjoy every precious moment.

About the Author

Brian Biro

—America's—
BREAKTHROUGH
Coach

Brian Biro is **America's Breakthrough Coach**! He is one of the nation's foremost speakers and teachers of **Leadership, Possibility Thinking, Thriving on Change, and Team-Building**. A major client described him best when he said, "**Brian Biro has the energy of a ten-year-old, the enthusiasm of a twenty-year-old, and the wisdom of a seventy-five-year-old.**" A former vice-president of a major transportation corporation and the author of 8 books including bestseller, *Beyond Success!,* Brian was **rated #1 from over 40 Speakers** at 4 consecutive INC. Magazine International Conferences. With degrees from Stanford University and UCLA, Brian has appeared on Good Morning America, CNN's Business Unusual, and the Fox News Network and as a featured speaker at the Disney Institute in Orlando. He lives with his wife Carole and daughters Kelsey and Jenna in Asheville, NC.

Acknowledgments

One of the secrets to discovering a truly joyful spirit is to stop for a moment each day and fill with gratitude for the tremendous people who have made immense, lasting contributions to your life. *It's Time for Joy* is a co-creation of dear friends, mentors, and teammates whose wisdom, example, and energy fill every page.

I thank Margie Hylkema for the loving support she gave me from the beginning to the end of this project. The irrepressible Raphiella Adamson provided her amazing energy every step of the way, lifting my confidence and sharing her empowering faith and belief in the value of this book.

I am incredibly fortunate to once again have worked with the best editor in the business, Karen Risch of Just Write. Not only is she exceptionally talented and conscientious, she is also great fun to work with!

The team at Morgan James Publishing, especially Ben and David Hancock, and Sherry Duke have given me invaluable support and guidance. They have created a new paradigm in publishing. I am so blessed to work with such a phenomenal creative team.

I thank my friend, Bob Proctor for his inspiration and excitement about applying *It's Time for Joy* principles, and Shore Slocum for helping me more fully understand that lasting happiness comes by creating "moments."

This book could not have been written without the immeasurable inspiration I have received from Larry Michel, Mark Segars, Helice Bridges, Eckhart Tolle, Lou Tice, Jamie Reeser, Scott Muir, Nick Daley, Doug Hanson, Daryl Kollman, Marta Carpenter, John Robbins, Kate Rander, Paulette Kimura-Shimabukuro, Mother Teresa, Mahatma Gandhi, John Wooden, Lynda Cormier, Katlin Hecox, and my mother and father, Miriam and Louis Biro.

Finally I want to express the inexpressible—the love and appreciation I feel for the three people who constantly fill my life with shining purpose—my wife, Carole, and my amazing daughters, Kelsey and Jenna.

With these remarkable friends, teachers, and family providing me with their inexhaustible love, motivation; wisdom, and faith, I truly feel like the happiest person I know!

Appendix:
Abundance Affirmations

These examples of Abundance Affirmations are provided as guides to help you create your own.

Spiritual

I intend to receive a growing, deepening spiritual awakening bringing me closer to God, to humanity, to my family, and to my true soul!

I know this is true because

- I take special time each day to quietly, joyfully, and lovingly thank God for the miracle of every precious moment.
- I have unstoppable determination to be the best person, husband, father, and example I can be.
- The pathway to peace is through connection with God's love and spirit!
- I am so grateful for God's loving favor!

Lifestyle and Balance

I intend to receive wonderful balance of family time, quiet contemplation time, creative time, and exercise time.

I know this is true because

- I have complete choice to make it so!
- Through this balance I am at my best as a husband, father, professional, and human being.
- Balance brings joy and peace of mind!

Finances and Abundance

In intend to receive such great success with my speaking and writing that we enjoy unstoppable abundance, sublime peace of mind, and complete financial freedom.

I know this is true because

- I love my work and believe deeply in its value and benefit to others.
- The sales of my books produce great residual income every month!
- My speaking is in huge demand as I easily book over 70 events this year!
- God flows through me with complete presence every time I speak!
- My clients are deeply moved, wildly enthusiastic, and truly inspired by my teaching and heart, generating awesome word of mouth business!
- I receive at least three calls or web inquiries for bookings every day!

Personal Growth

I intend to receive fantastic inner fulfillment, joy, and peace of mind from my unstoppable abundance thinking, attitude of gratitude, patience, and kindness.

I know this is true because

- I always seek to understand before seeking to be understood.
- I handle all challenges with easy humor, possibility thinking, and simple human kindness.
- I am committed to being the best possible example of character I can be for Carole, Kelsey, and Jenna.
- I joyfully surrender all ego, need for approval, and need to control others completely to God!

Health and Vitality

I intend to receive amazing energy, terrific fitness, and vibrant health that fill me with spirit, happiness, and enthusiasm every day!

I know this is true because

- I joyfully eat lightly, and healthfully with an abundance of super foods, fruits, and vegetables.
- I work out at least six days a week with focus, energy, and dedication.
- I comfortably keep my weight below 172 lbs.

Additional Resources from Brian Biro

If you would like information on Brian Biro's other resources, including his speaking, seminars, books, CDs, and products, please go to: www.brianbiro.com *or call 828-242-0738.*

Expand the joy with this special offer!

You'll receive over $2,300 of gifts and savings including:

- Over four hours of Brian Biro's *Breakthrough Stories* audios
- Brian's *Unstoppable Spirit* audio program (only available here!)
- Four life-changing *Special Reports*
- A $2,000 discount for your organization when they hire Brian for a live presentation

To access your gifts and savings opportunities go to:
www.itstimeforjoy.com

BUY A SHARE OF THE FUTURE IN YOUR COMMUNITY

These certificates make great holiday, graduation and birthday gifts that can be personalized with the recipient's name. The cost of one S.H.A.R.E. or one square foot is $54.17. The personalized certificate is suitable for framing and will state the number of shares purchased and the amount of each share, as well as the recipient's name. The home that you participate in "building" will last for many years and will continue to grow in value.

Here is a sample SHARE certificate:

HABITAT FOR HUMANITY

THIS CERTIFIES THAT

YOUR NAME HERE

HAS INVESTED IN A HOME FOR A DESERVING FAMILY

1985-2005

TWENTY YEARS OF BUILDING FUTURES IN OUR COMMUNITY ONE HOME AT A TIME

1200 SQUARE FOOT HOUSE @ $65,000 = $54.17 PER SQUARE FOOT

This certificate represents a tax deductible donation. It has no cash value.

YES, I WOULD LIKE TO HELP!

I support the work that Habitat for Humanity does and I want to be part of the excitement! As a donor, I will receive periodic updates on your construction activities but, more importantly, I know my gift will help a family in our community realize the dream of homeownership. ***I would like to SHARE in your efforts against substandard housing in my community!*** *(Please print below)*

PLEASE SEND ME ___________ SHARES at $54.17 EACH = $ $___________

In Honor Of: ______________________________

Occasion: *(Circle One)* *HOLIDAY* *BIRTHDAY* *ANNIVERSARY*

OTHER: ______________________________

Address of Recipient: ______________________________

Gift From: _______________ ***Donor Address:*** ______________________________

Donor Email: ______________________________

I AM ENCLOSING A CHECK FOR $ $_____________ PAYABLE TO HABITAT FOR HUMANITY OR PLEASE CHARGE MY VISA OR MASTERCARD *(CIRCLE ONE)*

Card Number ______________________________ Expiration Date: ___________

Name as it appears on Credit Card _________________ Charge Amount $ ___________

Signature ______________________________

Billing Address ______________________________

Telephone # Day ______________________ Eve ______________________

PLEASE NOTE: Your contribution is tax-deductible to the fullest extent allowed by law.

Habitat for Humanity • P.O. Box 1443 • Newport News, VA 23601 • 757-596-5553

www.HelpHabitatforHumanity.org